DON HARRISON

Charleston | London

THE
History
PRESS

Published by The History Press
Charleston, SC 29403
www.historypress.net

Front cover, clockwise from top left: Calvin Murphy, Naismith Basketball Hall of Famer from Norwalk. *Courtesy of Niagara University*; Wes Bialosuknia, UConn's outstanding long-range shooter in the mid-1960s. *Courtesy of University of Connecticut*; Yale's 1956–57 Ivy League championship team coached by Joe Vancisin. *Courtesy of Yale University*.

Back cover, clockwise from top left: Marcus Camby, All-NBA defender and University of Massachusetts All-American from Hartford. *Courtesy of Denver Nuggets*; John Williamson of New Haven, who starred on two ABA championship teams with the New York Nets. *Courtesy of New York Nets*; President Barack Obama seems to be tickled by Coach Jim Calhoun's comment during the 2010–11 national champion Huskies' visit to the White House. *Courtesy of University of Connecticut*.

First published 2011
Manufactured in the United States
ISBN 978.1.60949.083.6
Library of Congress Cataloging-in-Publication Data
Harrison, Don.
Hoops in Connecticut : the Nutmeg State's passion for basketball / Don Harrison.
p. cm.
Includes bibliographical references.
ISBN 978-1-60949-083-6
1. Basketball--Connecticut--History. I. Title.
GV885.72.C8H37 2011
796.32309746--dc23
2011039782

For Lauren, Luke and Patrick. With grandchildren I am thrice blessed.

OTHER BOOKS BY DON HARRISON

Connecticut Baseball: The Best of the Nutmeg State
25 Years Plus One: Recounting the Meteoric Rise of Fairfield Basketball

As Contributing Author

Inside Women's College Basketball: Anatomy of a Season
Inside Women's College Basketball: Anatomy of Two Seasons

Contents

CONTENTS

Foreword

This book was written by a man who loves sports. I know that better than anyone. Don Harrison is my brother-in-law. We've been connected at the hip through college sports and as brothers-in-law for more than forty years.

For whoever would care to know—probably no one—I've had a connection to intercollegiate athletics in Connecticut for almost fifty years. I was a student athlete at Fairfield University in the early 1960s, followed by a twenty-year career coaching baseball, then as an athletics director at three Connecticut colleges: Fairfield University, the University of Hartford and, most recently, Sacred Heart University, where I'm in my twentieth year.

Obviously, there was no way Don and I wouldn't cross paths, having shared the same footprint, albeit from different vantage points over all those years. As irony would have it, it was during a time when Don was covering Fairfield University's participation in the 1973 NIT that he met my sister, Patti, at a postgame celebration at Mama Leone's Restaurant in New York City. It was a love-at-first-sight encounter. Their love story compared to none.

Back to my charge writing a foreword to this book…

Don remembers more about Connecticut sports than anyone I know, albeit professional sports, college, high school or wherever else he finds a story in the Nutmeg State. For better or for worse, he knows more about my career in intercollegiate athletics than I care to remember.

Don is like a right-brain artist. He remembers and captures through his God-given gift of writing thoughts, feelings and reflections in real time, much the way an artist does with a paintbrush and canvas. That's the good news. The bad news is that he has the uncanny knack of remembering things I try to forget. His brain is like a trap. Anything that enters that frontal lobe never leaves, even if I wished it would at times. And just when I think there's a stat or an event that he couldn't possibly remember, he shocks me. He remembers every little detail as if it occurred just after breakfast this morning.

What he remembers and has on file about basketball in Connecticut is astounding. But that's not all. The truth be known, he has fervor for Major League baseball as well. His earlier book, *Connecticut Baseball: The Best of the Nutmeg State*, is a testimony to his passion for that game. Upon reading this edition, most people will agree that he has a special place in his heart for basketball in Connecticut, too.

For Don Harrison, most of the attractiveness about sports is derived from the variety of experiences they offer, combined with the encounters he has had covering them. Don caught most of it in a bottle. Hardly a major basketball event took place over a three-decade period that Don hasn't witnessed personally.

And it's not always about glory and the trophy. Fittingly, Don has always had a special place in his heart, which speaks volumes about him, to remember a sad event that on occasion accompanies sport. After all, it's easy to write about the champion or championship trophy.

One such gut-wrenching experience was the story you will read about Ray Andrade, who was shot and killed in an attempted holdup of a small grocery store on Madison Avenue in Bridgeport. Ray was a schoolboy point guard, starred for Tom Penders at Bridgeport Central and led the Hilltoppers to the 1970 Class L state championship game against Hillhouse. He made second team All-State as a sophomore—and never played an organized game again. This piece by Don was cited in *The Best American Sportswriting 1993*.

No one is better qualified to write about some of the most colorful events and personalities associated with basketball in Connecticut than Don. He has a state, a regional and even a nationwide reputation as an award-winning sportswriter with a gifted perspective about the characters and personalities he has covered or otherwise come in contact with in the profession. If there ever were a writer who could lift a personality right off the page, it's Don.

Probably no book better captures the spirit and soul of basketball and its influence on the Nutmeg State than this one. Harrison has gathered many of his noteworthy features and columns that appeared in the *New York Times*, the *Sporting News*, *New Haven Register*, *Waterbury Republican-American*, *Fairfield County Advocate*, *Fairfield Citizen-News*, *Bridgeport Light*, *Fairfield* (University) *Now* and *Sacred Heart* magazine. There is some new material that readers will enjoy, too.

Few books about Connecticut sports feature more greatness than stories about people who made a lasting impression on our state. The book is worthwhile for a wider audience, too, because it so aptly describes the humanness, decency, successes, failures and heart of its characters. Basketball fans will be saddened when the book ends.

Hoops in Connecticut: The Nutmeg State's Passion for Basketball is a superb book, lively and fascinating, and one that entertains and, in some measure, educates. Everyone interested in sports—especially in the rich tradition of college basketball in Connecticut—should read this book.

Over the years, I was privileged to witness and, in some instances, experience firsthand many of the real-life stories about which Don writes. Hardly a basketball story warranting publication eluded Don's attention in this book. No one is more capable of anchoring this material in authenticity and detail.

Don writes about some of the most colorful basketball personalities ever assembled in the Nutmeg State, maybe anywhere. So shut off the television. Turn on a reading lamp. Find a comfortable chair. Settle down for a special trip. And when finished, you'll feel you relived some of the most exciting stories ever written about sports in Connecticut.

C. Donald Cook
Executive Director of Athletics
Sacred Heart University

Acknowledgements

J eff Saraceno, commissioning editor at The History Press, was
remarkably supportive throughout the many stages of this project, and
I thank him for this many times over.

I also wish to thank William J. Pape II, publisher of the *Waterbury
Republican-American*—and my former employer—for granting permission
to reproduce photos that appeared in his Pulitzer Prize–winning
newspaper. I am appreciative of the research assistance from Michael
Dooling, the newspaper's librarian, as well.

I thank Tom Kabelka, the now-retired chief photographer at the
Republican-American and a longtime friend, for allowing me to reproduce
his photos.

Joan Seirup, wife of retired Roger Ludlowe High School Coach Bob
Seirup, was kind enough to gather photographs from her husband's
scrapbook. Three former coaches—Bob Saulsbury, John Castellani and
Bob Baroni—shared their personal photos, as did a former athlete and
coach, Alvin Clinkscales. Thanks to all.

Susan Gunn-Bromley, curator of the Norwalk Museum, supplied the
image of Calvin Murphy from his days at Norwalk High School. Frank
Corr, a retired Norwalk middle school history and geography teacher (Rita
Williams was among his students), loaned several of his NBA player cards.

I am indebted to more than a dozen college sports information offices
and their directors, both present and past, for providing images of players
and coaches. Thanks go to: Thomas Pincince, Central Connecticut

State University; Kyle Muncy, Mike Enright and the late Joseph Soltys, University of Connecticut; Rick Bender, Dartmouth College; Matt Plizga, Duke University; Jack Jones and Ray Van Stone, Fairfield University; Daniel Ruede and Sam Angell, University of Hartford; Jason Feirman, Louisiana State University; Andy Beardsley, University of New Haven; Derick Thornton, Niagara University; Charles Wiseman, Ohio University; Arthur Parks and Christopher Magnoli, Providence College; Bill Peterson, Sacred Heart University; Eric Coplin, St. Anselm College; Jason Behenna, Seattle University; and Steve Conn and Peter Easton, Yale University.

Four National Basketball Association teams supplied photos, too. I thank Tim Galt and Dan Tolzman, Denver Nuggets; Kevin Grigg and Megan Heineman, Detroit Pistons; Dan Smyczek and Nicole Carnemolla, Milwaukee Bucks; and Patrick Rees and Devin DePoint, New Jersey Nets.

Gary Johnson of the NCAA office in Indianapolis filled in several blanks, and many sports information directors were helpful in that capacity, too, notably David Kingsley, Trinity College; Brian Katten, Wesleyan University; Jon Litchfield, High Point University; Mike Warwick, Ithaca College; and John Dodderidge, Rockhurst University.

I thank Bart Fisher, the retired sports editor of the *New Britain Herald*, for sharing his expertise—most especially the contact information for John Castellani. Tom Chiappetta, executive director of the Fairfield County Sports Commission, was helpful in a similar vein; the commission's 2011 ballot included the name of a man, Tom Callahan, who was, in all probability, the first Connecticut native to play in the NBA.

Introduction

If memory serves, I was fourteen years old when I was able to palm a basketball for the first time. But little did I realize that Dr. Naismith's game would forever hold me in its grasp.

Bank shot. Hook shot from the corner. Push shot from the left of the key. Those were my weapons of choice as a teen, and I put them to use wherever and whenever there was a game. At Art Concilio's backyard court on French Avenue. At Hugh Klockars's side-yard court on Frank Street. At the Union School playground. On Jackie Bruno's court in front of the oversized garage where his father housed his oil trucks.

On a few occasions, we ventured into the center of town to the Barkers' court, which attracted the best players East Haven had to offer. Billy Barker, my teammate on the Old Stone Church team, held the home court advantage here.

Throughout the fifties, basketball was *the* game in the shoreline community of East Haven, Connecticut. Our revered high school coach, Frank Crisafi, assembled teams that never seemed to lose; they played a tight two-three zone, ran the weave with precision and rarely took a bad shot.

In a glorious five-season span (1953–57), the Yellow Jackets, as they are known, won 118 games and lost just 5. Yes, 5. Included in the mix were a Connecticut-record 77-game winning streak, three Class M state titles (1954, '55 and '57) and one New England championship (1954) at the old Boston Garden. Tony Massari, one of the superb high school marksmen of the era, who later played at Harvard, was the star of the 1953–54 champs.

The coach would prefer to forget two of those five defeats, but they were memorable. In the state championship game of the 1952–53 season, Lyman Hall of Wallingford came from behind in the final minutes to eke out a 48–47 win at Yale's Payne Whitney gym. "We" had won all twenty-two games prior to that evening.

Three years later, East Haven's record winning streak ended in storybook fashion—again in the Class M state title game, again at Yale—when an angular six-seven center with a crew cut, Wayne Lawrence, scored 38 points, and Stonington walked off the court with a 62–60 victory over Crisafi's squad. (Lawrence became an all-Southwest Conference player at Texas A&M and was oh-so-close to making the Boston Celtics when Russell, Heinsohn, Cousy, et al., wore the green and white.)

Outside the confines of East Haven's snug basketball court, the game was being played at higher levels. One of my classmates, Bob Schneider, had access to tickets for Yale games; his dad worked at the university. On a few occasions, Schneider, another Bob, Gilson and I were transported to New Haven, where we watched the Elis play Columbia, Penn or another Ivy League institution.

Yale, coached by Howard Hobson, was quite formidable in those days. Its marquee player, Johnny Lee, would appear on the cover of *Sports Illustrated*'s January 21, 1957 issue, and his teammates Eddie Robinson and Larry Downs were also first rate. Columbia, though, had a diminutive All-American guard named Chet Forte, and I recall the night he scored thirty points, sinking twenty of twenty-one attempts from the foul line to spark the Lions' victory. The date was January 18, 1956. You can look it up in the *ESPN College Basketball Encyclopedia*.

When I was in my early teens, my father took me to the old Madison Square Garden on Eighth Avenue for the first time to watch the New York Knicks. Joe Lapchick was the coach, and Carl Braun, Dick McGuire, Nate "Sweetwater" Clifton and Harry "the Horse" Gallatin were the players who made the Knicks click.

My dad pointed to a man who seemed to be seated in a booth above the court. "That's Marty Glickman," he told me. "He's broadcasting the game on the radio."

Wow. What a great way to make a living, I thought. "Good, like Nedicks," Glickman would intone whenever a Knick scored but never when a Neil Johnston or a George Mikan put the ball into the hoop.

14

Many, many jump shots later, I would sit next to Glickman at courtside during the still-prestigious National Invitation Tournament. *Waterbury Republican* sports editor and hall of fame sportscaster side by side. We made small talk, and now I wish I had mentioned that special moment when my father pointed him out to me.

On the afternoon of November 4, 1996, I witnessed another side of Glickman. At this juncture, I was working in public relations at Sacred Heart University, a burgeoning institution of higher learning in Fairfield, Connecticut. Although established by the Diocese of Bridgeport, it was the first Catholic college in the nation to be led and staffed by the laity.

Glickman was part of an all-star lineup assembled by Rabbi Joe Ehrenkranz, co-founder of the university's Center for Christian-Jewish Understanding (CCJU), for a memorial tribute to Mel Allen, his rabbi, friend and longtime "voice" of the New York Yankees. The ecumenical service took place at St. Patrick's Cathedral in New York City.

Glickman and another hall of fame sportscaster, Curt Gowdy, were front and center with Cardinal John O'Connor, Sacred Heart president Anthony J. Cernera, PhD, and Arthur Richman, senior adviser to Yankee owner George Steinbrenner. (Arthur, whom I had corralled to participate in the service, had been one of my mentors at the *New York Mirror* some three decades earlier.) Suzyn Waldman, still a Yankee broadcaster, shared her vocal talents with the assemblage by performing the National Anthem and "America the Beautiful."

Glickman spoke of Mel Allen's fairness. "I respected Mel's ability to root for the other guy. How could you root against Ted Williams? How could you root against Bob Feller? In the World Series, Stan Musial? He was a baseball fan first, a sports fan who believed in fair play and sportsmanship."

I digress. In September 1960, I joined the *Mirror* sports staff in an entry-level position—copyboy. My duties included striping the sports news from the AP and UPI teletype machines and placing the text in the night sports editor's "in" basket, then rolling up the edited copy and placing it in a canister for its journey through the pneumatic tube to the composing room, where it would be set in type. I also answered the phone, gathered photos and clips from the morgue upstairs and once each evening made a food run to the A&M Restaurant across the street or to another nearby bistro.

There were perks, though. The Garden offered complimentary tickets for most of its events, and I snatched them up whenever I had a free evening. Tuesday and Wednesday were my nights off.

The Knicks were a lesser team at this stage, but our comps placed us in the row directly behind their bench. This was basketball heaven. Richie Guerin, Willie Naulls and jumping Johnny Green did their best to earn a victory for New York; alas, they were outclassed on most nights by the Lakers of Baylor and West, the Royals of Robertson and Twyman, the Celtics and just about everybody else.

On one occasion, I passed along my Knicks tickets to my dad and younger brother, Harry, who got to savor Elgin Baylor's NBA-record seventy-one-point night at the Garden.

In March 1961, I was able to secure seats for three sessions of the National Invitation Tournament, all featuring Providence College. I rooted for the Friars because the superb guard Johnny Egan, late of Hartford Weaver, and four other Nutmeggers—George Zalucki of Hartford Public, Carl Spencer and Tim Moynahan from Waterbury and Dennis Guimares of New Haven—wore PC's black and white.

Egan was dominating in Providence's victories over DePaul, Niagara and Holy Cross, the latter in overtime, but he was usurped by a tow-headed teammate, sophomore guard Vinnie Ernst, in the finale against St. Louis. PC prevailed, 62–59, and Ernst was voted the NIT's Most Valuable Player. On campus, he became known as "Valuable Vin."

In the spring of 1962, I earned a promotion to sports deskman, and now I was editing copy, writing headlines and supervising the page makeup in the composing room. (Only union printers were permitted to touch the metal type.) When the Hearst Corporation stunned 1,600 employees by shutting down the *Mirror* in mid-October 1963, our legendary sports columnist, Dan Parker, pointed me in the direction of his hometown newspaper, the *Waterbury Republican.* I was hired, virtually on the spot, and began to cover high school sports and share the deskwork.

In December, I was presented my first college assignment, and truthfully, it was a trip to enter the Payne Whitney gym for the first time as a member of the Fourth Estate. Yale, led by an undersized, high-scoring forward, Rich Kaminsky, defeated Holy Cross, 83–68, on that Saturday evening.

I would make the lengthy drive to Storrs twice the following December, the first for the debut of Wes Bialosuknia, a heralded sophomore guard who was reputed to be able to score from the outer reaches of the Field House. Wes lived up to his pedigree with 20 points and six-eight senior Toby Kimball took down 28 rebounds as UConn dispatched American International, 98–67. A touch of irony: AIC's high scorer that evening was an aggressive sophomore named Jim Calhoun, who finished with 27 points. Hmmm, what ever happened to him?

Just prior to Christmas, I watched Bialosuknia generate 25 points to spark the Huskies to a hard-earned 70–67 decision over Fordham. "He's the best shooter I've seen at Connecticut," Rams Coach Johnny Bach stated, "and that goes back to 1953."

At this juncture, UConn and Yale dominated college basketball in the Nutmeg State; everybody else competed at the College Division or small college level. Enter a bespectacled attorney named George Bisacca, who held down two part-time positions at Fairfield University: athletic director and basketball coach. George had big ideas, even with a nickel-and-dime budget.

Few fans outside the metropolitan Bridgeport area were aware, or even cared, when Bisacca's Stags were reclassified major college in basketball prior to the 1964–65 season. His teams had dominated the old Tri-State League against the likes of Adelphi, CCNY and Bridgeport, and now he and his Jesuit squad were ready for bigger game. Our new sports editor, Milt Northrop, assigned me to cover Fairfield's home game against Providence on January 4, 1965.

Coach Joe Mullaney's Friars, who would assemble a 24-2 won-lost record and garner a number four ranking in the final AP and UPI national polls, were a prohibitive favorite. Led by Jimmy Walker, a sophomore guard with remarkable skills, PC possessed so much front-line talent that Mike Riordan, later a solid professional with the Knicks and Baltimore Bullets, rarely made the starting lineup. And yet Fairfield—sparked by Connecticut kids named Jim Brown, Mike Branch and Pat Burke—was able to rally from a fifteen-point deficit to tie the score at sixty-one with four minutes, forty-two seconds to play. The capacity crowd's deafening support shook the tiny campus gym.

Yes, Providence ultimately prevailed, 72–65, but now I knew where I wanted to be on winter evenings. I was hooked on the college game.

For the next sixteen seasons, I would have press-row seats at Fairfield, UConn and Yale, at the Hartford Civic Center, the old New Haven Arena and the New Haven Coliseum and occasionally at Madison Square Garden, the Palestra, the Providence Civic Center and other basketball vistas of note.

I don't recall the year, but I do remember one trip to Storrs that was scary. Entering the recently constructed Route 84 in Waterbury, I pulled into the passing lane and began to accelerate. Something—or someone—told me to return to the slow lane. I did. And just after I completed the maneuver, a car heading in the opposite direction whizzed past us. Incredible. We would have been killed. After spending a few moments at the side of the road to collect our wits and thank our lucky stars, we proceeded on our journey to UConn.

Fairfield, under a new coach, Fred Barakat, finally achieved its NIT goal in 1973 and made repeat appearances in 1974 and 1978. UConn, guided by a new man, Dee Rowe, made successive trips to the NIT in 1974 and 1975 and reached the Sweet Sixteen in the 1976 NCAA Tournament. Tony Hanson, who had developed his game on the playgrounds of Waterbury and at Holy Cross High School, was the cornerstone of the latter two Husky squads.

Dom Perno, a New Haven native, Wilbur Cross High All-Stater and former UConn captain, succeeded Rowe as head coach in 1977, and he was at the helm when the Huskies made a successful entry into the Big East Conference.

Yale began to emerge from its doldrums during the 1978–79 season by upsetting a Corny Thompson–Mike McKay UConn team and stunning a Joe DeSantis–Mark Young Fairfield squad on the road.

Because of the NIT and the Holiday Festival, I had the opportunity to chronicle many of the era's greatest collegiate players from outside the Nutmeg State, too. Pistol Pete Maravich, Walt Frazier, Jo Jo White and even a seven-foot UCLA center known as Lew Alcindor appeared in the Garden as underclassmen.

On the game's professional side, I was at press row for two noteworthy events, separated by just a few weeks, in 1972: the Lakers' four-games-to-one triumph over the Knicks in the NBA championship series and then the second NBA-ABA All-Star Game, the latter played at the Nassau Coliseum in Uniondale, New York. The NBA won, 106–104, but the upstart ABA, led by Julius Erving, Rick Barry and Artis Gilmore, proved that it belonged on the same court with its well-established brethren.

This is a scene from the author's bachelor dinner, but the subject must have been basketball. *From left*: Fred Barakat, Don Harrison and Porky Vieira. *Courtesy of Tom Kabelka.*

From a personal standpoint, the 1973 NIT represents a landmark occasion in my life. Florence Barakat, wife of the Stags coach, introduced me to Patricia Alice Cook Lawrence—sister of Fairfield's young athletic director, C. Donald Cook—at the tournament dinner in Mama Leone's. This was just hours after Fairfield had upset Marshall, one of the favorites, by an 80–76 score in the opening round.

Patti and I met again, quite by chance, four nights later at a postgame alumni gathering in New York. From that point, just six months would elapse before we exchanged wedding vows at St. Mathew's Roman Catholic Church in Norwalk, Connecticut. In basketball terms, this can be defined as a carefully orchestrated fast break. For nearly forty years, Patti has endured my passion for basketball with good grace (for the most part). I thank her for our three children and for all the richness she has brought to my life.

I trust you will enjoy this labor of love. The contents of *Hoops in Connecticut: The Nutmeg State's Passion for Basketball* reflect my personal journey as sportswriter, sports editor, freelance writer and magazine editor and, as such, do not purport to be encyclopedic in scope. However, even I might win games coaching a team composed of the players within these pages.

Let's see: Calvin Murphy and Johnny Egan will start in backcourt, we'll place Vin Baker at center and Charles Smith and Tony Hanson are the forwards. Super John Williamson will be the first guard off the bench, and several other notables are available when needed.

We've got next.

CHAPTER 1

Basketball

IT'S CONNECTICUT'S GAME, TOO

G ive the Commonwealth of Massachusetts its due. The game of basketball was invented by a young physical education instructor named Dr. James Naismith at the YMCA's International Training School in Springfield, Massachusetts.

The Canadian-born Naismith (1861–1939) was seeking an indoor sport suitable for play during the harsh Massachusetts winters for the school's eighteen students. He wanted to create a game of skill for the students instead of one that relied solely on strength. The first game of "basket ball" was played on December 21, 1891, with a soccer ball and two peach baskets used as goals.

Eureka! From such humble beginnings sprang a sport that is now played by countless numbers of men and women worldwide and ranks second, behind soccer/football, as the world's most popular spectator sport.

If basketball had its humble origin just a handful of miles away from the Connecticut border, it is safe to say the state of Connecticut has done more than its New England brethren to nurture the game and lead it to new heights. Consider:

- The University of Connecticut is the first, and still only, New England institution of higher learning to win more than one NCAA national championship in men's basketball. The Huskies, as any UConn aficionado will tell you, prevailed in 1999, 2004 and 2011, the latter following an improbable eleven-game run through the Big East and NCAA Tournaments. All three titles

All-American guard Kemba Walker completes the traditional cutting down of the net following UConn's stunning 53–41 victory over Butler for the 2010–11 NCAA national title—the Huskies' third since 1999. Walker was selected by the Charlotte Bobcats as the number nine pick in the 2011 NBA draft. *Courtesy of University of Connecticut Athletic Communications.*

were achieved under the leadership of a Hall of Fame coach, Jim Calhoun.

- The UConn women, coached by another Hall of Famer, Geno Auriemma, supplanted Tennessee as the dominant women's program by capturing seven national titles, all since 1995. They also won ninety consecutive games—surpassing the UCLA men's record of eighty-eight straight.

- Sacred Heart University of Fairfield became the first New England school to win the NCAA Division II national championship. The Dave Bike–coached Pioneers defeated Southeast Missouri State, 93–87, in the 1986 title game played in, of all places, the Springfield (Massachusetts) Civic Center.

- The first official intercollegiate game was played between Yale University and Wesleyan University on December 10, 1896, in New Haven. Wesleyan won by a score of 4–3.
- Connecticut high schools dominated the old New England Interscholastic Tournament, winning twelve of the last thirteen titles and twenty-six of thirty-seven events overall. Often, two Nutmeg State teams would meet in the finals. The tournament was established by Tufts College in Medford, Massachusetts, in 1921 and was shifted to several sites until it found a "permanent" home in the old Boston Garden in 1945. Crowds often taxed the Garden's capacity of thirteen thousand. A near-riot that took place in the closing seconds of the 1958 championship game between Wilbur Cross of New Haven and Somerville, Massachusetts, led Connecticut to withdraw from the tournament four years later.

Basketball's hold on the Nutmeg State is demonstrated in many ways. When *Sports Illustrated* selected the fifty greatest sports figures of each state for the twentieth century, no fewer than thirteen basketball players made its Connecticut list. Norwalk's Hall of Fame guard, Calvin Murphy (no surprise), placed third, behind 1972 Olympic decathlon champion Bruce Jenner of Newtown and the runner-up, quarterback Steve Young of Greenwich, the 1995 Super Bowl MVP.

Other cagers on *SI*'s best-of-the-twentieth-century Connecticut log were Vin Baker of Old Saybrook (thirteenth), Jen Rizzotti of New Fairfield (sixteenth), Marcus Camby of Hartford (twenty-first), Nykesha Sales of Bloomfield (twenty-second), Mike Gminski of Monroe (twenty-fifth), Michael Adams of Hartford (twenty-ninth), Charles Smith of Bridgeport (thirty-seventh), Rick Mahorn of Hartford (thirty-ninth), Chris Smith of Bridgeport (forty-second), Scott Burrell of Hamden (forty-third), John Bagley of Bridgeport (forty-sixth) and John Williamson of New Haven (forty-ninth).

One can quibble with Williamson's comparatively low ranking—his pro career exceeded that of Messrs. Burrell, Bagley and Chris Smith—but there are omissions of note, too. Where is Hartford's Johnny Egan, the clever guard who became the first of the Nutmeg State's NBA stars? Where is Bridgeport's Wes Matthews? New Haven's Tracy Claxton, a two-time All-American at Old Dominion University and the MVP of the women's 1985 Final Four?

UConn in the pros.
Top row, left: Ray Allen, 1999 Upper Deck; *right*: Scott Burrell, 1998 Fleer.
Bottom row, left: Caron Butler, 2003 Topps. *right*: Ben Gordon, 2008 Topps.

Top, left: Donyell Marshall, 2005 Topps; *right:* Emeka Okafor, 2005 Bowman.
Middle, left: Richard Hamilton, 2005 Topps; *right:* Toby Kimball, 1973 NBA Properties;
Bottom: Clifford Robinson, 2004 Topps. *Courtesy of Frank Corr and the author.*

The Long and the Short of It, a documentary shot in the mid-1950s, co-starred Frank "Porky" Vieira, the five-six Quinnipiac College guard who averaged 32.8 points per game, and seven-one Wilt Chamberlain, then a teenage sensation at Overbrook High School in Philadelphia. *Courtesy of University of New Haven Athletics Communication.*

Where, indeed, is the inimitable Florindo "Porky" Vieira, who, at five-six or so, may have been the greatest little man to play a game geared to the elongated? Vieira *averaged* 32.8 points per game across four seasons at then-tiny Quinnipiac College in the 1950s and, as a semi-pro, once generated 89 points—without benefit of the 3-point shot—in a single game.

Alas, compilations of all-time anybodies are subjective and gosh-awful imperfect.

As the lone Connecticut native elected as a player to both the Naismith Memorial Basketball Hall of Fame and the National Collegiate Basketball Hall of Fame, Calvin Murphy is the clear choice as the Nutmeg State's greatest. Who's number two? One can make a case for the aforementioned Camby, Gminski, Baker and Williamson.

The six-eleven Camby, an All-Stater at Hartford Public, is one of the NBA's premier defensive players of this era, starring with the New York Knicks and four other teams across fifteen seasons. As a junior at the University of Massachusetts, he led the 1995–96 Minutemen to thirty-one consecutive victories before they bowed to Kentucky, 81–74, in the National Semifinals. Few were surprised when he was voted NCAA Player of the Year.

Gminski, who also stands six-eleven, grew up in the Bridgeport suburb of Monroe and became best known as a scoring big man, from Masuk High School (40 points per game as a senior) to Duke (two-time All-American and three-time *Academic* All-American) and then during fourteen years (1980–94) in the NBA. He averaged 11.7 points with the New Jersey Nets, Philadelphia 76ers and two other clubs.

Yet another man of six-eleven stature, Baker was a late bloomer at Old Saybrook High School and drew little attention from college scouts. He elected to play at the University of Hartford, where, after a freshman season languishing on the bench, he developed into a star, ranking among the nation's scoring leaders as a junior (27.6 points per game) and senior (28.3). Selected by the Milwaukee Bucks as the eighth pick in the 1993 NBA draft, Vin became a first-rate professional from the outset, appearing in four straight All-Star games (1995–98). He concluded his thirteen-year NBA career with a 15.0 scoring average.

Williamson was called "Super John" for good reason. The six-two guard was a marvelous scorer at New Haven's Wilbur Cross High School (averaging nearly 40 points per game as a senior), at New Mexico State University (a school-record 27.2 points per game for two seasons) and as a pro. Across eight seasons in the NBA and ABA, his scoring average was 17.5 points—a performance exceeded by only one man with Connecticut ties: Calvin Murphy. Williamson died of kidney failure related to diabetes on November 30, 1996. He was just forty-five years old.

Hartford native Marcus Camby soars to reject a shot. With the Denver Nuggets, Camby led the NBA for three straight seasons (2006, 2007, 2008) in blocks per game. *Courtesy of Denver Nuggets.*

A multitude of Connecticut products have distinguished themselves at the collegiate level. According to the voluminous *ESPN College Basketball Encyclopedia*, published in 2009, no fewer than six Nutmeg State natives were selected as the all-time Best Player at their respective college or university—the aforementioned Murphy at Niagara and Baker at Hartford, Michael Adams (Hartford) at Boston College, Rick Mahorn (Hartford) at Hampton, Charles Smith (Bridgeport) at Pittsburgh and Sly Williams (New Haven) at Rhode Island.

Chosen as all-time Fan Favorites were John Bagley (Bridgeport) at Boston College, Ryan Gomes (Waterbury) at Providence, Walter Luckett (Bridgeport) at Ohio University and Williamson at New Mexico State.

As one might guess, all of these athletes were named to the encyclopedia's all-time Top Five at their respective institutions. And so were the late Gus Broberg (Torrington) at Dartmouth; Camby at UMass; Jay Murphy (Meriden) at Boston College; Chris Smith (Bridgeport) and the late Walt Dropo (Moosup) at UConn; Paul McCracken (Hillhouse of New Haven) at Cal State–Northridge; Bill O'Connor (Stamford) at Canisius; Tyrone Canino (Hartford) and Howie Dickenman (Norwich) at Central Connecticut State; Courtney Alexander (Bridgeport) at Fresno State; Mark Noon (Bristol) and Peter Egan (West Hartford) at Hartford; Bob Nash (Hartford) at Hawaii; Jared Jordan (Hartford) at Marist; Porky Vieira (Bridgeport) at Quinnipiac; Kenny Green (Waterbury) at Rhode Island; Doremus Bennerman (Bridgeport) at Siena; and Chris Dudley (Stamford) at Yale.

Not surprisingly, Sacred Heart University of Fairfield, a commuter school until the early

Bob Baroni, who was Mike Gminski's coach at Masuk High School, joins his former protégé for his induction into the Jackie Robinson Professional Wing of the Fairfield County Sports Commission Hall of Fame in 2007. *Gene Cayer / Courtesy of Bob Baroni.*

28

Basketball

1990s, placed four Connecticut residents on its all-time Top Five—Ed Czernota (Bridgeport), Tony Judkins (Hartford), Keith Bennett (Stamford) and Roger Younger (Middletown).

A COACH YOU MAY NOT KNOW

During the many months of research for this project, I learned of a Connecticut native whose success as a collegiate coach rivaled many of the so-called greats—but was uncommonly brief. John Castellani, who was born and raised in New Britain, coached for just two seasons at Seattle University, capping the second year by leading the Chieftains to the 1958 Final Four, where they lost to Kentucky and the legendary Adolph Rupp in the championship game.

Of course, it didn't hurt that Seattle's finest player was Elgin Baylor, a Consensus All-American, the first pick in that year's NBA draft and a future Hall of Famer.

Castellani admits that, when he was hired as coach and athletic director in 1956, he had not yet heard of Baylor, who was an incoming transfer student from the College of Idaho. "Years ago in the fifties, there was very limited communication. There weren't any scouts, not like there are now," he said. "I was easily converted to Baylor-ism. He was Michael Jordan before there was Michael Jordan."

The short, fiery coach—who had been an assistant at Notre Dame, his alma mater, prior to his hiring at Seattle—and the gifted Baylor were to share in forty-five victories in fifty-four games during their two seasons together.

In 1956–57, the Chieftains won eighteen consecutive games before bowing to St. Bonaventure, 85–68, in the NIT quarterfinals at Madison Square Garden, finishing 22-3.

Baylor, a sophomore, was astounding in his debut, leading the nation in rebounding (20.3 per game) and ranking third in scoring (29.7). "He was a guy who was a leader on and off the court. You couldn't help but like him," Castellani said of Baylor.

The next year, Seattle won four straight NCAA Tournament games and found itself in the title game against Kentucky. Unfortunately for the Chieftains, they would meet the Wildcats in Louisville's Freedom Hall—

John Castellani, the New Britain native who coached Seattle University to the 1957–58 NCAA National Championship game, with his All-American forward, Elgin Baylor. Castellani was an invited guest at Baylor's Basketball Hall of Fame induction in 1977. *Courtesy of John Castellani.*

just a ninety-minute drive from the UK campus. Castellani's integrated team was hardly the fan favorite among the crowd of 18,803. "The only African Americans in the building were the four on my team," he noted.

Although Baylor, whose 32.5 scoring average would place him second in the nation behind Cincinnati's Oscar Robertson, was hindered by a broken rib incurred in the team's 73–51 semifinal upset of Kansas State, Seattle led Kentucky by 11 points in the first half. The Chieftains still were on top, 60–58, with some seven minutes to play. But Baylor, struggling to breathe at times and playing the second half with four fouls, was unable to contend with the Wildcats at the end. Seattle lost, 84–72, to complete a 23-6 season.

"I always said we had the best team; we didn't have the best coach," said Castellani, who later relocated to Milwaukee and became an attorney. "I had coached fifty-four games. Rupp had coached six hundred."

A month or so after the championship game, the Seattle program was rocked by scandal, and Castellani resigned after the Chieftains were given a two-year NCAA Tournament ban for recruiting improprieties. It was determined that the young coach had violated the rules by providing airfare to a neutral meeting point for a pair of recruits. "I probably crossed the line," Castellani admitted.

He turned the Chieftains over to Vince Cazzetta, his assistant coach and childhood best friend from New Britain. Cazzetta oversaw the program for five productive seasons and led Seattle to three NCAA Tournament appearances and a 94-39 record.

Cazzetta would resurface as head coach of the Pittsburgh Pipers in the fledgling American Basketball Association, guiding the team— featuring Hall-of-Famer-to-be Connie Hawkins—to the 1967–68 championship in his lone season at the helm. He was voted ABA Coach of the Year. He resigned when the team owners refused to grant him a raise to help in the relocation of his wife and six children to Minnesota, where the Pipers were moving. (They would return to Pittsburgh after just one season.)

Castellani had one more coaching stop remaining, too. Unable to find another job in the college ranks, he used his connection with Baylor as a selling point and became coach of the Minneapolis Lakers for 1959–60. He was dismissed in mid-season, as the NBA team, with Baylor hampered by injuries, stumbled to an 11-25 start.

"I got fired ten days before the [team] plane crashed into a cornfield," Castellani said. "Fortunately, nobody was killed."

Castellani and Cazzetta are among just five Connecticut natives to have coached in the professional ranks. The most recent, and still active, is Tom Thibodeau—yet another New Britain native. Thibodeau was chosen as 2010–11 NBA Coach of the Year after leading the Chicago Bulls to their first division title since the Jordan era and tying the record for most wins, with sixty-two, by a rookie coach.

The others? After retiring as a player, Hartford native Johnny Egan coached the Houston Rockets for three and a half seasons (1972–76), and Bob Staak, the former UConn long-range shooter and Darien native, was interim coach for one game with the 1997 Washington Bullets.

PENDERS AND OTHER COACHES OF NOTE

Tom Penders, a man I've known as an athlete and coach for forty-plus years, is the antithesis of Castellani in length of service. The Stratford native and former UConn two-sport athlete coached at the Division I level for thirty-three seasons (1974–2010), assembling a 594-420 record with Columbia, Fordham, Rhode Island, Texas, George Washington and Houston. Including earlier stops at two high schools (Bullard-Havens Tech and Bridgeport Central, three seasons, 59-10) and Division II Tufts (three seasons, 54-18), Penders was a head coach for a remarkable thirty-nine years. His combined record was 707-448.

He is now coauthor, with Steve Richardson, of his autobiography, *Dead Coach Walking: Tom Penders Surviving and Thriving in College Hoops*.

It would be difficult, perhaps impossible, to name all other native Nutmeggers who coached major college basketball. Some of the most prominent, with their cumulative won-lost records, are:

- Gerry Alaimo, of Torrington, nine seasons at Brown, his alma mater, 88-145.
- Dave Bike, of Bridgeport, thirty-three seasons at Sacred Heart, his alma mater, 505-462 (including one NCAA national title and twenty-one years at the Division II level).

- George Bisacca, of Fairfield, ten seasons at Fairfield, 151-87 (encompassing six years at the Division II level).
- Howard Cann, of Bridgeport, thirty-five seasons at New York University, his alma mater, 409-232.
- Howie Dickenman, of Norwich, fifteen seasons at Central Connecticut State, his alma mater, 236-208.
- The late Hugh Greer, of Suffield, sixteen-plus seasons at Connecticut, his alma mater, 286-112.
- Jack Kvancz, of Bridgeport, seven seasons at Catholic University, 64-116 (including two years at the Division II level).
- Nick Macarchuk, of Norwich, twenty-eight seasons divided among Canisius, Fordham and Stony Brook, 374-428.
- Glen Miller, of Groton, ten-plus seasons divided between Brown and Pennsylvania, 138-151.
- Reggie Minton, of Bridgeport, one season at Dartmouth and sixteen seasons at Air Force, 161-311.
- Bob Nash, of Hartford, three seasons at Hawaii, his alma mater, 34-56.
- Bill O'Connor, of Stamford, six seasons at Seattle, 72-87.
- Dom Perno, of New Haven, nine seasons at Connecticut, his alma mater, 139-114.
- Jack Phelan, of West Hartford, eleven seasons at Hartford, 128-181 (the first three years were at the Division II level).
- Steve Pikiell, of Bristol, six seasons at Stony Brook, 73-108.
- Bob Staak, of Darien, ten seasons divided between Xavier and Wake Forest, 133-155.
- Joe Vancisin, of Bridgeport, nineteen seasons at Yale, 206-242.
- Bob Zuffelato, of Torrington, ten seasons divided between Boston College and Marshall, 154-121.

Three of these gentlemen—Bike, Dickenman and Pikiell—were active head coaches entering the 2011–12 season.

Although Connecticut has yet to become home to a National Basketball Association franchise, many teams have played regular-season games here. As a sportswriter, I chronicled a handful of Boston Celtics games at the Hartford Civic Center in the late 1970s, and as a boy, I watched a few NBA games at the old New Haven Arena in the 1950s. That latter was made possible by the close association between the NBA commissioner, Maurice Podoloff, and the man who operated the arena, Nate Podoloff. They were brothers.

Minor league professional basketball in the form of the Eastern League flourished in Hartford and New Haven for a while in the 1960s. Gene Conley, perhaps best known as a six-foot-nine Major League pitcher, played for the Hartford Capitols, and Al Cervi, who had coached the Syracuse Nationals to an NBA title, guided the New Haven Elms in the first half of the 1966–67 season.

On the women's side, the Connecticut Sun brought the Women's National Basketball Association to the Nutmeg State in 2003. They play home games at Mohegan Sun in Uncasville.

CONNECTICUT'S ALL-TIME BEST PLAYERS

PLAYER & HOMETOWN	PRO CAREER	G	FG	PCT.	3-PT	PCT.	FT	PCT.	ASSTS	REBS.	PTS.	PPG
G—Calvin Murphy, Norwalk	1970–83	1002	7247	.482	10	.139	3445	.892	4402	2103	17949	17.9
G—Johnny Egan, Hartford	1961–72	712	2089	.429	--	--	1343	.805	2102	1284	5521	7.8
G—John Williamson, New Haven	1973–81	516	3724	.458	25	.234	1544	.826	813	722	9017	17.5
G—Michael Adams, Hartford	1985–96	653	3257	.415	949	.332	2158	.849	4209	1900	9621	14.7
G—John Bagley, Bridgeport	1982–94	665	2359	.437	114	.241	970	.779	3980	1729	5802	8.7
G—Wes Matthews, Bridgeport	1980–90	465	1463	.478	36	.225	692	.788	1955	625	3654	7.9
F—Vin Baker, Old Saybrook	1993–2006	791	4692	.485	39	.215	2416	.638	1509	5867	11839	15.0
F—Charles Smith, Bridgeport	1988–97	564	2993	.475	18	.194	2103	.774	798	3246	8107	14.4
F—Ryan Gomes, Waterbury	**2005–**	**450**	**1857**	**.448**	**330**	**.357**	**802**	**.800**	**699**	**2174**	**4846**	**10.8**
C—Marcus Camby, Hartford	**1996–**	**890**	**3622**	**.468**	**16**	**.193**	**1673**	**.678**	**1716**	**8903**	**8933**	**10.0**
C—Mike Gminski, Monroe	1980–94	938	4208	.465	6	.122	2531	.843	1203	6480	10953	11.7
C—Rick Mahorn, Hartford	1980–99	1117	3098	.493	5	.132	1562	.704	1082	6957	7763	6.9

Bold indicates active players, with statistics through the 2010–11 NBA season.

CHAPTER 2

The Players

ALEKSINAS BUILDING UP FOR FINAL UCONN SEASON, NBA

The basketball player of yesteryear was called Bones or Spider. One presumes he was called late for supper as well. He was more giraffe than athlete, all spindly arms and legs. No muscles to speak of, but those pointed elbows could be menacing.

We had Bones McKinney and Spider Bennett, and then there was Johnny Horan, the University of Dayton forward, circa 1955. He stood six-eight and weighed all of 185 pounds. They called him the "Vertical Hyphen."

Well, the day of the skinny-minny player is just about over. Now the sport is played by mastodons like Darryl Dawkins and Bob Lanier. Brawny men who are nearly as wide as they are tall, whose strength is comparable to their agility.

Brawny men such as six-eleven, 256-pound Chuck Aleksinas.

On some summer evenings, you are apt to find Aleksinas at the Nautilus Health Fitness Center in Colonial Plaza. There are no backboards or free throw circles here. Inside this storefront are a row of Nautilus equipment and a running track, on which young men (and some young women) build up their bodies and stamina. Aleksinas's eighteen-inch biceps strain against the machines. It is an impressive sight.

"I come here about twice a week to lift weights and run," he said. "I avoid free weights. I don't want to get too bulky; I want to be flexible.

"At Kentucky, we lifted very heavily. I think we lifted more than the football team. After my freshman year there, I started to like it. It gives you endurance; it's better for your heart."

Chuck's one and a half seasons at Kentucky started on a high—as a freshman, he was a member of the Wildcats' fifth NCAA national championship team, appearing in twenty-eight games and averaging 3.5 points—and ended after thirteen games and an 11.5 scoring average as a sophomore.

The Big A is building up for his second and final year in a University of Connecticut uniform, for a season that, if successful enough, could place him high up in the NBA draft. First-round draft choices have been known to require Purolator trucks to transport their bonus money home.

A stronger, more mobile Aleksinas may be too much center for any UConn opponent to handle, Georgetown's elongated freshman, Patrick Ewing, notwithstanding. These steamy evenings in the Nautilus Health Fitness Center figure to prove worthwhile.

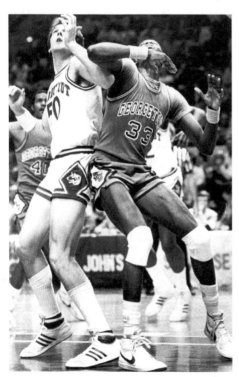

Perhaps some of Aleksinas's motivation is derived from a junior season that did not quite measure up to expectations. On some occasions, especially against Big East and other top-flight competition, this man-child from the hills of Morris could be immense. Twenty-seven points against Providence? Fine. Twenty-five in a regionally televised one-point decision over St. John's? Super. Twenty-four against Western Kentucky in the finals of the Connecticut Mutual Classic? Great. Twenty against Syracuse and Villanova? No complaints there.

Chuck Aleksinas of UConn contests a rebound with Georgetown's Patrick Ewing. *Courtesy of University of Connecticut Athletic Communications.*

He made some all-star teams (Widmer All-East, *Basketball Weekly* All-East, U.S. Basketball Writers' All-New England), and he set a New England record for field goal percentage (63.1), which shaded the 62.9 established by Fairfield's six-ten Mark Young in 1977–78.

So a lot was good.

But then there were less-productive, indifferent performances, in scoring and in rebounding, against some of the lesser teams on the Huskies' 1980–81 schedule. The bottom line on the Big A's first season at Connecticut was a decent, but less than awesome, 13.8 scoring average and 7.0 rebound average. The team finished 20-9 but lost 4 of its last 5 games.

"I wasn't really pleased," he admitted. "I could have rebounded better. A lot of games I said I was going to get every rebound in sight, and I'd get a lot. I had my best games against the best teams. I know I had a problem getting up for the weaker teams. Like a Manhattan when they had a center six-five. As a team, we played well at times. We played poorly at times. Overall team consistency was a problem. We should," he said with conviction, "do it every game, or at least most of the time."

Aleksinas speaks candidly about his comparatively modest scoring average. You can't score when you don't get the ball, and there were some nights when it seemed that few passes came in his direction.

"If you're shooting 63 percent and taking eight shots [he averaged 8.4 field goal attempts per game], it's not what you want. It's not what the team wants," he said. One can surmise that Aleksinas will shoot with greater frequency as a senior.

The former Wamogo Regional High School All-Stater is keeping his shooting eye sharp this summer, of course. He's just returned from two weeks at Lefty Driesell's basketball camp, competing with and against the likes of John Lucas, Phil Chenier, Maryland-bound Adrian Branch and "a lot of people you've never heard of, that can play." Recalled the Big A: "It was 110 degrees down there. It was tough playing the first week."

Closer to home, you'll find Aleksinas lofting feathery jump shots in the Pearl Street Summer League, with a team called Teddy's Den. Sometimes the opposition is less than inspiring, but at least it's an opportunity to play in a well-run summer league.

It's another opportunity, too, to prepare for that final season at UConn and the spot he covets on somebody's NBA roster. "I definitely want to play pro, and the biggest thing I have going for me is my size," he said.

"[Seven-footer Wallace] Bryant of San Francisco is the only center I know of who figures to go high in the draft. There are other good centers in college, but they'll be forwards in the NBA. It looks good for me."

Aleksinas won't be the only member of the 1981–82 UConn team to be drafted—All-East forward Corny Thompson is another certainty and Mike McKay is a strong possibility—but he could become the first athlete from Greater Waterbury to play in the NBA. And that would be something big.

Waterbury Sunday Republican, July 26, 1981

BAGLEY COURTS YOUNGSTERS

It's called the Bagley-Walden Foundation. As in John Bagley, NBA point guard, and Karl "Bucky" Walden, point guard-turned-personnel-director. Their nonprofit organization was formed in July 1988 to help the young people who roam Bridgeport's streets, the kids who loft jump shots and slam dunks in the playgrounds and are in need of a role model.

John Bagley, who survived the mean streets and dark alleys of Father Panik Village to become an All-State guard at Warren Harding High, an All-Big East point guard at Boston College and a solid pro with the Cleveland Cavaliers and New Jersey Nets, cares. He is a walking, breathing example of a street kid turned caring adult.

"My mother, Nellie May Bagley, was involved with community services like the Multi-Service Center, ABCD. She got me to understand the need to create and provide for your own people," Bagley explains.

"I grew up on the East Side in Father Panik. I came across some situations that tend to creep into your own family. Peer pressure. There was a little involvement with my family and friends. Nobody else was doing anything, so I decided to lay my reputation on the line."

Walden's basketball prowess was evident at Central—"I was the point guard on the 1974–75 state championship team"—and at Ohio University, but today he earns his livelihood as the personnel manager for the Private Industry Council of Southern Connecticut. "I don't play competitively anymore," he says. "I made a decision to get involved with the administrative end."

The foundation's goals, short- and long-term, are to provide opportunities, athletic and otherwise, for inner-city youth, kids whose futures are in jeopardy because of alcohol or drug abuse, illiteracy, dropping out of school and myriad other problems.

Declares Walden: "Drugs and the lack of educational motivation are destroying the hope of Bridgeport's inner-city youth."

Says Bagley: "The foundation allows us more room to do what's necessary, to become a strong institution within the community."

Some of their programs, such as basketball leagues for grammar school kids and high school girls, won't become a reality until next year. An NCAA-sanctioned league for college-age players and beyond is also on the 1990 drawing board.

John Bagley drives for two points against the Washington Bullets. *Courtesy of Nets Basketball.*

Other programs are in place this year, notably a two-day Superstar Basketball Clinic on August 19–20 at the University of Bridgeport. "The theme for the clinic is Back to School, Stay in School," Walden says. "It worked like a charm last year.

"Working with Bill Flynn and Mike Bisceglia, we have a long-term agreement with UB. This includes a summer league and educational program."

UB's Harvey Hubbell Gym is also serving as the site for Bagley's Summer Basketball Camp, which is taking place this week. Profits from this venture, according to Walden, will go to the foundation's "entertainment and reading programs."

Underprivileged kids are benefiting, too. A bank, Citytrust, and businesses such as Cola-Cola, Crystal Rock Water Co., Arctic Sports Shop and Popeye Chicken are sponsoring their attendance at the camp.

The Players

For kids who perform well in the classroom, the foundation rewards them with a bus trip to the Meadowlands Arena to watch Bagley and his Nets teammates play. There were eleven such trips to Nets games this past season, involving Multicultural Magnet, High Horizons Magnet, Longfellow, Winthrop, Read and other schools.

"The kids got to meet Nets players, pose for a picture at center court," Walden recalls.

The youngsters' favorite Nets player, John Edward Bagley, is assessing his own NBA future at this juncture. A three-year contract assures the twenty-nine-year-old guard of employment, but little else is certain. Lester Conner, a six-four journeyman, supplanted the former Harding star in the starting lineup during the season, and now the club has acquired Oklahoma's All-American point guard, Mookie Blaylock, in the college draft.

After three straight seasons of consistent double-figure scoring and challenging for the NBA assists leadership, Bagley saw his production dip markedly, to a 7.4 scoring average and 391 assists. Conner, with appreciably more playing time, averaged 10.3 points and led the club with 604 assists.

What happened, and more to the point, what's going to happen?

"I was playing well before I got sick," John explains. "I had a bad cold and became anemic; it made me weak. Conner played well when he got the chance. I've got to give him credit."

And next season?

"Starting isn't the most important thing. Every role is important," Bagley says. "Unless you're a Kareem [Abdul-Jabbar], you have to prepare yourself for coming off the bench. You've got to play well in a backup role; it could help you to start if the guy in front of you falls down.

John Bagley, 1990 NBA Properties card. *Courtesy of Frank Corr.*

"I love the game. I plan to harvest the crop as long as I can."

Regardless of his role next season, John Bagley won't allow a repeat of last year's abysmal 26-56 record—an exercise in futility exceeded only by the NBA's expansion clubs, Charlotte and Miami, and the Los Angeles Clippers (hello, Charles Smith).

"On paper, we were a lot better than we showed," Bagley says. "Looking at what we had, losing was tough for me. Somewhere along the line, something was missing. I'm a winner. I play to win."

On the court. With the kids on Bridgeport's mean streets.

"Wes Matthews made me a believer. We can all make it in some way," he says. "That's why I came back. Kids can reach out and touch it. There's so much more we can do."

Bridgeport Light, July 12, 1989

Rising Star Already a Big Name at Camp

Vin Baker was on a roll. He was sinking jump shot after jump shot from the outer reaches of the Old Saybrook High School gym. Four in a row. Five. Six.

A rotund man wearing glasses was retrieving the basketball for Baker, delivering soft bounce passes to the six-eleven Milwaukee Bucks forward as he traversed an imaginary circle about twenty-five feet from the basket. Seven in a row. Eight. Nine. His next attempt seemed true but—clank—bounced harmlessly off the rim. The streak was over.

"I'll bet," somebody said, gesturing toward the man under the basket, "those were the first passes he ever threw."

Baker repeated the words to the man, Walter Luckett, and then doubled up in laughter. Luckett, who is Baker's friend, confidant and agent, laughed too. "Hey, that's pretty good," he said with a soft smile.

In an earlier time, Luckett would have been the day's focal point, the recipient of those soft bounce passes. He was one of the nation's most prolific shot makers in the early 1970s at Kolbe High School in Bridgeport, a schoolboy All-American who accumulated 2,691 points—still a Connecticut record. His likeness appeared on the cover of *Sports Illustrated* in 1973, and he became an All-Mid-American Conference star at Ohio University and a second-round draft choice of the Detroit Pistons.

But this was July 1996 and the opening day of the third annual Vin Baker Hoop Camp, the first of the daily sessions where 124 boys and 6 girls gathered to learn the rudiments of the game and rub elbows with a hometown National Basketball Association star. Perhaps as many as 35 youngsters attend the camp on scholarship, courtesy of Baker's and Luckett's largesse.

Unlike some professional athletes, who make cameo appearances at the sports camp that bears their name, Baker is a daily presence in Old Saybrook. At one moment he is exchanging small jokes with a camper, the next providing hands-on instruction.

"I enjoy getting around and helping them one on one. They want to feel important, just as they make me feel important," Baker said in a soft, well-modulated voice. "I want them to see a role model they can trust and believe in. The main thing, I want these guys to become better people."

The camp's location, in the gymnasium and on the grounds of his

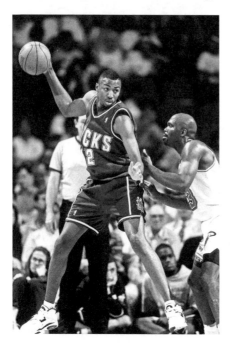

Vin Baker, who grew up in the shoreline community of Old Saybrook, muscles his way toward the basket with the Milwaukee Bucks. *Courtesy of Milwaukee Bucks.*

former high school, is important to Baker. "My parents still live about five minutes from here. This is where it all began," he said. "I love being back in the high school."

An only child, Vincent Lamont Baker spends a portion of the summer with his parents. His mother, Jean Baker, has worked at Chesebrough-Ponds for thirty years and is a quality assurance processor auditor. His father, the Reverend James Baker, is an auto mechanic and a Baptist minister.

The link between Baker and Luckett, the former star who is now director of community relations with Chesebrough-Ponds, goes back more than a decade. He met Vin and his mother at a company picnic.

When Vin Baker was a small boy?

"He was never small," Luckett replied, smiling.

Their friendship flourished, from early shooting contests at Chesebrough-Ponds picnics through Baker's four-year career at the University of Hartford, where he rose from virtual unknown into an All-American center coveted by the NBA. It was Luckett, recalling his own missteps about leaving college a year early to turn pro, who urged Baker to remain at Hartford for his senior year.

Today, Luckett and an associate, Lou Albanese, are Baker's representatives. Three years ago, when Baker was the number eight selection in the NBA draft, they negotiated the original ten-year, multimillion-dollar contract with

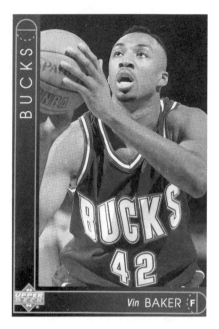

Vin Baker, 1994 Topps card. *Courtesy of Frank Corr.*

the Bucks. They've since assisted with a new, more lucrative arrangement.

"My whole focus in basketball is Vincent. I feel very blessed to have a tremendous guy in Vincent," Luckett said.

One would assume the Bucks have similar feelings. At the tender age of twenty-four, Baker enjoys the status as one of the NBA's finest—if underrated—forwards. In the 1995–96 season, he was Milwaukee's leading scorer (21.1) and rebounder (9.9), both figures placing him among the top fourteen players in the league. Consistency personified, he led the Bucks in scoring forty-one times and was first in rebounding on fifty-four occasions. For the second straight year, he played in the NBA All-Star Game. "It's funny," Baker said. "As soon as I got to that level of competition, my game got better."

He's also remarkably durable. Baker has yet to miss a regular-season game, and two years ago he topped the NBA in minutes played with an average of 41.0 per game. He was fifth in that category last season with 40.5 minutes a game.

After three NBA seasons, Baker's productivity exceeds that of any other Connecticut-bred athlete—Calvin Murphy and John Williamson notwithstanding. Across 246 games with the Bucks, he has amassed 4,286 points and a 17.4 average.

At a similar stage in his career, the Norwalk-born Murphy, who is widely regarded as the finest player produced in Connecticut and is a member of the Basketball Hall of Fame, had 3,790 points and a 15.7 average. Williamson, from New Haven's Wilbur Cross High School, amassed 3,215 points and a 14.1 average in his first three years with the New York Nets of the American Basketball Association.

Luckett predicts ever greater heights for his protégé, labeling Baker "the best power forward, considering his promise, in the game. He's a six-eleven Scottie Pippen."

Baker, who played in comparative obscurity at Old Saybrook High and at Hartford and is just now beginning to receive acclaim, agrees: "Pretty soon, people are going to know who Vin Baker is."

Of course, the youngsters who flock to his camp already know. "He's a really big name around here," says Nicole Corbin, a twelve-year-old camper who will be a seventh grader at Eliot Middle School in Canton.

Jason Carrafiello, a seventeen-year-old senior-to-be at Luckett's old high school in Bridgeport, needed little encouragement to return to Baker's camp for the second year. "He works with me on an individual basis, he's given me more confidence," Carrafiello said. "You can tell he likes to work with kids. He's fun to be with."

Robert Hall, fifteen, who attends the Full Gospel Tabernacle Church in Old Saybrook, where Baker's father is the assistant pastor, has been in the camp since its founding. In Vin Baker, he's found somebody he can look up to—both literally and figuratively. "He's somebody you can always talk to," Hall said.

New York Times, August 11, 1996

REMEMBERING A QUANTUM LEAPER

In the era of the quantum leap, Mike Branch was the quantum leaper. When Fairfield University basketball made the climb to the NCAA major college ranks in the mid-1960s, the six-three Branch epitomized the comparatively unknown Stags: too small to compete at the game's highest level but too talented and too determined to be denied.

In eighteen seasons of chronicling college basketball, from Madison Square Garden to the Palestra to the Providence Civic Center, I never saw another player rebound with Mike's tenacity and skill. He was capable of out-leaping centers and forwards several inches taller; even a seven-footer, Art Beatty of American University, came out second best under the backboards in their 1966 meeting.

In my mind's deepest recesses, this memory persists: Branch, more than three feet off the floor, is tapping in a rebound against St. Peter's in the old Garden. Everyone else on the court seems rooted in *terra firma*.

George Bisacca, the coach, athletic director and practicing attorney who was the architect behind Fairfield's remarkable basketball transition, always lamented Mike's lack of positioning. "He'd never box out, but he always got the ball because he wanted it more than anybody else," Bisacca said. "Mike was a killer rebounder."

The numbers support Bisacca's contention. In two seasons against major college opposition, Branch ranked eighth nationally in rebounds per game in 1964–65 (16.0) and seventh in 1965–66 (16.6). You may recognize some of the names above him: Rick Barry, Elvin Hayes, Wes Unseld and Toby Kimball. And some of those below: Cazzie Russell and Clyde Lee, both All-Americans, and seven-footer Henry Finkel.

Branch came to Fairfield from Hillhouse High School in New Haven, an All-State center who was enticed by Bisacca's promise to elevate the university's basketball program to Division I. He was joined by a lesser-known youngster from Hartford Public, Pat Burke, with whom he would co-captain the 1965–66 squad.

As sophomores, they weathered the team's final season in the College Division ranks, providing notable victories over Boston College (in Bob Cousy's coaching debut) and Fordham en route to a 14-11 record. Mike reached his pinnacle as a scorer that winter with a 21.2 average and pulled down a school-record 404 rebounds (16.2)—still the single-season high thirty years later.

The leap to Division I took place the following season, and Branch was instrumental in early wins over Fordham, Seton Hall and Canisius before running afoul of academic requirements. Nonetheless, the Stags' 14-7 record was deemed highly creditable and provided an appropriate steppingstone for the future.

The Players

Many longtime Fairfield followers still insist that, with the probable exception of the 1977–78 squad, the 1965–66 team remains the program's best. Seniors Branch and Burke were joined by juniors Jim Brown, Charlie Phillips and Billy Pritz and sophomores Bill Jones and Art Kenney, and this nucleus was capable of compiling an imposing 19-5 record.

After an opening loss to nationally ranked St. Joseph's in the old New Haven Arena, Fairfield roared through the remainder of December and all of January without another defeat. Talented Boston College was upended at Chestnut Hill. The Stags outlasted St. Peter's in triple overtime, swept Xavier, St. Francis of Pennsylvania and Duquesne on the school's first extended road trip and defeated Massachusetts, Holy Cross and Niagara at home.

As January turned into February, the Stags' thirteen-game winning streak had become the talk of eastern college basketball. Proclaimed the headline on a nationally syndicated feature: "A Minor Miracle Grows in Fairfield."

Mike Branch scores with a tap-in against St. Peter's in Madison Square Garden—Fairfield's first appearance in the mecca of college basketball, February 26, 1964.
Courtesy of George Bisacca.

Many of us have grim recollections of the occurrences in that distant February—Burke's tragic death in an off-campus accident and the team's snubbing by the National Invitation Tournament's selections committee. But we also remember, on a more joyful note, Branch's resounding finale in the campus gym—24 points and 24 rebounds in a 111–60 annihilation of Bridgeport, the partisan crowd chanting "We love Branch" in the game's waning moments.

All these memories resurfaced in December when I read of Mike Branch's passing at forty-nine. Kidney failure, it was said.

For the most part, his whereabouts following graduation in 1966 (BS degree in economics) were shrouded in mystery. He played semipro basketball in the Eastern League for a while and toured the nation with the Harlem Wizards, and then he was gone.

Bisacca remained loyal until the end. When Mike couldn't be located after being voted into the Alumni Association's Athletic Hall of Fame, the old coach was present to accept the plaque, in January 1984, for the player he regarded as "my flesh and blood." (Mike did appear on campus in 1993 for an on-court presentation.)

At the funeral services, conducted at the House of Prayer in New Haven, George and his wife, Millie, were among the mourners who witnessed a poignant farewell from one of the Branch children—Michael Jr.

Fairfield (University) *Now*, Winter 1995

CLINKSCALES'S GLOBETROTTING LEADS TO SHU

When the second battle of Park Avenue is staged Saturday night at UB's Harvey Hubbell gym, one onlooker will have ambivalent feelings. It is impossible for Alvin Clinkscales to take sides when Sacred Heart and Bridgeport are opponents on the basketball court. "When they play, I try to find a neutral zone and watch," he says, chuckling. "I don't want to show any favoritism."

For nearly eighteen years, this likeable, gregarious man has held a variety of administrative positions at SHU and currently serves as the assistant vice-president for community/minority affairs. His links with

UB go back even further—to the mid-1950s, when a rangy, six-five forward named Al Clinkscales was a small college All-American for the Purple Knights. Indeed, he was the school's first All-American.

No, he won't be rooting for either side Saturday when Sacred Heart tries to avenge the 106–105 defeat it incurred in January.

"I don't root for either one," he explains. "Bruce [UB coach Bruce Webster] is a real good friend of mine. Of course, I work here and Dave is a former player of mine. I just like to see good performances."

The "Dave" in reference is Dave Bike, the bear of a man who coaches the Pioneers. A quarter of a century ago, a Clinkscales-coached Notre Dame High School team was undefeated through twenty-three games before it encountered one of the greatest Hillhouse High squads in

Alvin Clinkscales, *right*, with Harlem Globetrotter teammate Meadowlark Lemon. *Courtesy of Alvin Clinkscales.*

the championship game of the Class L state tournament. The Lancers featured a rugged center named Dave Bike and a five-nine All-Stater, Rodock Cox, who could out-leap players nearly a foot taller. "That was my best team," Clinkscales says, "and that was the only game we lost."

If one were to select a basketball all-star team from the Park City, it would be difficult to exclude Alvin Terrence Clinkscales. From the late 1940s until well into the 1960s, he was an imposing figure whenever he performed—at Central High School, Arnold College and UB, with the Harlem Globetrotters and the semipro Milford Chiefs. Shoot, he even teamed up with a pair of All-Americans, La Salle's Tom Gola and Duquesne's Sihugo Green, on a Fort Dix team that won back-to-back U.S. Army championships.

Frank "Porky" Vieira, who was a sophomore teammate on Central's 1950 New England Championship squad and later a frequent opponent in the semipro ranks, summed up Clinkscales's attributes thusly: "Al was the [Bill] Russell of the 1950s, a zone by himself."

Before shot blocking became the rage, Clinkscales was an intimidating presence on the court, a player who forced opponents to alter the trajectory of their missiles or, on occasion, bypass the opportunity for fear of rejection. He was the primary defensive force on the Central team that ruled New England.

"I was the rebounder on that team. Me and a kid named Gene Bethea. Ronnie DelBianco was our big scorer, and Ernie Pettruciano was our ball handler," he recalls. (Vieira, not yet a star, came off the bench to score points.) "Would we have been successful today? Everything is relative. It's hard to project them into this era. Inside my own head, I think we'd be able to compete. We'd do fine."

The Hilltoppers, who were coached by one of the city's legends, the late Eddie Reilly, had fallen one point short in the state championship game against New Britain. But nobody was their equal in Boston Garden, not even the Somerville, Massachusetts team led by Ron Perry—the father and namesake of the recent Holy Cross All-American.

Clinkscales says, "They hadn't seen the black athlete in that area. The difference in the game was the board strength."

He recalls the Hilltoppers winning the championship game "by five." But some other memories were less pleasant. "The cops had to take us up the elevator [in Boston Garden]. And we needed a police escort out of town the next day."

Clinkscales as a Sacred Heart University administrator. *Courtesy of Alvin Clinkscales.*

At tiny Arnold College in Milford, Alvin began to perfect the offensive side of his game against some formidable opponents such as Seton Hall's seven-foot Walter Dukes and Zeke Zawoluk, the St. John's All-American. When Arnold was incorporated into UB, he found himself as the senior co-captain of the 1953–54 Purple Knights, a season in which he averaged 21 points and 14.7 rebounds and was selected to the NAIA All-American team. "Coach [Herb] Glines made me a scorer. Taps, drives, short stuff."

After graduation, Clinkscales was faced with two basketball choices: a tryout with the New York Knicks or the Harlem Globetrotters. In deference to his mother, he opted for the latter, although "I had no doubt I could have made [an NBA] club."

The two years with the Globetrotters were enriching, especially from a travel standpoint. Night after night, game after game, he clowned to the strains of "Sweet Georgia Brown" throughout the South and West. "When I was in the circle, I never enjoyed it," he admits. "Clowning wasn't my forte."

Of his roommate, Meadowlark Lemon, he recalls an ambitious man who "always wanted to be what he got to be—a big star."

In that era, the Globetrotters possessed enough talent to prove a match for the NBA's best in exhibition games. Clinkscales relishes his memories of playing against the St. Louis Hawks with Bob Pettit and Cliff Hagan and the Minneapolis Lakers. It took a call from Uncle Sam to end his 'Trotter career.

Alvin's army experiences brought him into contact with athletes from many different walks of life—baseball's Sandy Koufax and Don Drysdale, pro football's Roosevelt Grier ("He sang at my wedding") and Sherman Plunkett and such basketball notables as Gola, Green, Wally Choice and Al Ferrari. So talented was his army team that they lost just once in two years.

After the service, he returned to the Bridgeport area, married an attractive woman named Peggy Holmes and began to raise a family. Today, all three children are grown: Keith, twenty-six, holder of a Harvard MBA and publisher of a magazine called *Urban Profile*; Norma, twenty-three, a senior at Howard University; and Erik, twenty-two, a junior at Sacred Heart.

In 1958, Notre Dame High School welcomed Alvin Clinkscales as its first boys' basketball coach—a distinction accompanied by his becoming the first black head coach of a high school team in Connecticut. Al's successful reign ended a decade later when he became a full-time administrator, first at the high school and then across the street at Sacred Heart.

"People ask me: 'Do you miss it?' I tell 'em 'no.' I have no interest in coaching basketball anymore," he says. "Basketball was something that worked out well for me, and I knew when it was time to walk away."

Each of the area's four-year schools—SHU, UB and Fairfield—beckoned in the intervening years when there was a coaching vacancy. Always his answer was the same. He'd prefer to watch from a distant vantage point, as he will do on Saturday night.

Bridgeport Light, February 21, 1990

EGAN SET THE STANDARD FOR NUTMEGGERS

Johnny Egan wasn't the first.

Tom Callahan, of Stamford, a three-sport athlete at Rockhurst, a small Jesuit college in Kansas City, Missouri, is believed to be the first player with Connecticut roots to play major league basketball. Callahan, a six-one guard, appeared in thirteen games with the Providence Steamrollers of the Basketball Association of America, precursor to the NBA, in the league's inaugural season, 1946–47.

Two other Nutmeggers, the late Bobby Knight of Hartford and Worthy Patterson, the New Haven-born, Greenwich-reared guard who was the inspirational leader of three UConn Yankee Conference championship teams in the early 1950s, also reached the NBA prior to Egan. Knight, who also performed with the Harlem Globetrotters, played two games with the 1954–55 New York Knicks. Patterson's cup of coffee with the

1957–58 St. Louis Hawks encompassed four games. Both men were hampered by the color barrier that existed in the NBA of the 1950s.

But if John Francis Egan wasn't the first, he was the first Connecticut guy to carve out a substantive career in the NBA, putting in eleven seasons (1961–72) with the Detroit Pistons, New York Knicks, Baltimore Bullets, Los Angeles Lakers, Cleveland Cavaliers and San Diego–Houston Rockets. He was an important complementary guard for the Chamberlain-West-Baylor Lakers, who were NBA runners-up in 1969 (to the Celtics) and 1970 (to the Knicks).

However, a freak knee injury, incurred in his dorm room in the fall of his junior year at Providence College, cost Egan some of the explosiveness and spring that he exhibited at Weaver High School and as a PC sophomore. His hang time on drives to the basket had earned him the nickname "Spaceman."

JOHNNY EGAN
guard

LOS ANGELES

Johnny Egan, 1970 Topps card. *Courtesy of the author.*

"I think I lost some of my jumping ability. I never performed the way I could have after that," Egan admits. "I played in the pros on one leg."

When he was recruited by PC coach Joe Mullaney, Johnny Egan already was a New England legend, a charismatic five-eleven guard who provided the spark to lead Weaver to back-to-back Class L state championships and the 1957 New England scholastic championship.

In the New England finals at Boston Garden, Egan converted a pair of free throws with no time on the clock to send the game into overtime and then scored 12 points in the three-minute overtime to lift the Beavers to the title. He finished the game with 36 points—perhaps the greatest individual performance in the history of the tournament.

Although Lenny Wilkens, who was a year ahead of him at Providence, would have a better career in the pros, Egan was the Friars' first "name"

Left: Egan, from Hartford Weaver, became one of Providence College's all-time stars and an NBA guard for eleven seasons. *Courtesy of Providence College Media Relations.*

Right: Egan's jersey is retired as part of the Friars Legends Forever tradition in February 2009. *Courtesy of Providence College Media Relations.*

recruit, the player who arrived with the most acclaim. And he delivered as a sophomore, averaging a team-high 20.9 points en route to propelling the Friars to a fourth-place finish in the then-prestigious National Invitation Tournament at Madison Square Garden.

Despite the loss of some mobility, Johnny averaged 14.2 points as a junior, and the Egan-Wilkens backcourt carried PC to the 1960 NIT championship game, where it bowed to Bradley and Chet Walker, 88–72.

As a senior captain, though, Egan was the catalyst behind the 1960–61 Friars winning the NIT for the first time. He averaged 18.8 points, a mark punctuated by a 34-point performance in the 73–67 decision over DePaul in the tournament's opening round. He also delivered big in subsequent NIT wins over Niagara and Holy Cross, the latter in overtime. In the championship game, a pro-PC capacity crowd of 18,496 looked on as the Friars edged St. Louis, 62–59. For the second time in three years, he was chosen to the All-NIT team. Many old-line PC fans will recall people lining Route 6 from the Connecticut border all the way into downtown Providence, where an estimated ten thousand people welcomed the champs back home.

Selected by the Pistons as the twelfth pick of the 1961 NBA draft, Egan embarked on a well-traveled pro career, playing with the dregs of the league as well as Laker teams with three all-time greats in the lineup. He reached a personal peak in 1963–64, the season in which he was traded to the Knicks, averaging 13 points and 5.4 assists. The latter figure placed him fifth in the league.

After eleven years as a player and three and a half seasons as the Rockets coach (129-152), Egan entered the insurance business and made it big. He married his high school sweetheart, Joan Grimaldi, who was a member of the Weaver cheerleading squad, in 1964. They settled in the Houston area and had two children, John Jr. and Kimberly. Joan died of ovarian cancer more than a decade ago.

"My wife used to say, 'You had a charmed life growing up, because everyone patted you on the back because you won,'" Egan recalls. "It's true. We were really, really blessed."

STANDOUT ATHLETE, COMPASSIONATE INNER-CITY PRINCIPAL

The irony is not lost on some visitors. A black-and-white photograph of the principal appears in the athletic trophy case at Warren Harding High School in Bridgeport. He stands self-consciously, arms placed behind his back, among a group of six young men. His gaze is both shy and noncommittal. Emblazoned on his jersey are the word "AMITY" and the numeral "25."

Many Harding students recognize their principal in this photo of the *New Haven Register*'s 1964 Class A All-State Team, although Ed Goldstone was a lot huskier—and twenty-eight years younger—when he played for Amity Regional High School in Woodbridge.

Dr. Edward Charles Goldstone smiles when the photo is mentioned. "The photograph is here because a Harding athlete, Jack Kvancz, is in it," he explains. "Yes, some of the students recognize me in the photo.

Some were aware of my athletic background." He smiles again. "I never set foot on the court here. My record is the mystique of it."

On the surface, Ed Goldstone's presence as principal of this inner-city school located on the east side of an economically troubled city seems a contradiction. It doesn't compute. He is a golden boy, Yale-educated, pristine and suburban. Bridgeport is grimy and urban, a city in which murder and drug deals are rampant, a community in which auto thefts rank fifth nationally on a per-capita basis.

Why *is* Ed Goldstone here? One gathers he wouldn't want to be anyplace else.

"Before we get settled, let's take a walk through school," he tells a visitor. We stroll through the Harding corridors on a crisp winter morning, pausing only briefly for Goldstone to visit a classroom and chat with a teacher. The students in the room are orderly and attentive. The halls are noticeably devoid of graffiti.

"I wanted you to see that teachers are teaching and students are learning," he says as we return to his office on the first floor.

Warren Harding and the other public high schools, Bassick and Central, are beacons of light in this downtrodden city, perhaps the last hope for many young people. They—along with two parochial schools, Kolbe Cathedral and nearby Notre Dame in Fairfield—represent opportunity for Bridgeport's teenagers. Equipped with knowledge, they will progress in society; to drop out means a life spent in menial jobs or, worse, succumbing to the lure of the streets.

"We try to motivate students to continue through four years of high school. We see high school as their door to the future," Goldstone says. "There's a great attrition rate; we lose a lot of students from freshman through senior year.

"I am very concerned with urban education. I do see hope for Bridgeport once the economy turns around, but realistically, that's not going to happen until the end of the year. Without employment, you're going to see social problems in the city and they're going to affect the students."

Goldstone, who arrived at Harding in 1986, after several years as assistant principal at Sheehan High School in suburban Wallingford, doesn't envision himself as a savior. But many of those who work for and with him speak of the man in reverential tones.

"The principal we had before was a blunder and thunder kind of guy. Ed Goldstone is very low key. I really love the guy; I like to work with him," says Francis Kryzwick, a social studies teacher now in his twentieth year at Harding.

Some critics call him "Easy Ed" and claim he's too laidback. But others believe his low-key demeanor is ideal in a potentially volatile situation.

"He's a very hard worker, a very visible administrator," points out Bob Cole, the school's athletic director and football coach. "You'll catch him in the hallways and in the classrooms. The kids all know him. All the athletes are aware of his background in sports."

Charlie Bentley, the highly acclaimed coach who has directed the Harding boys' basketball team to seven state championships in the past fourteen seasons, describes Goldstone as "fair and consistent. He challenges the kids and teachers to be better. He has a standard he wants everyone to live up to."

Anne Giroux, whose tenure as a Harding English teacher embraces twenty-seven years, says Goldstone "practices a philosophy in the pursuit of excellence. He maintains a school atmosphere conducive to learning and achievement."

Always Reaching

"Pursuit of excellence." This phrase seems to capture the essence of Ed Goldstone's being, from the very beginning.

Remember Chip Hilton, the fictional athlete who sprang from the mind—and pen—of the late Clair Bee? In Bee's enduring series, Hilton threw fifty-yard touchdown passes, scored thirty points in basketball games and hit tape-measure home runs. He was also modest, straight arrow and unfailingly polite. In the 1950s and early '60s, every boy (or so it seemed) aspired to be Chip Hilton.

Chip Hilton could have been a model for Ed Goldstone. At Amity Regional, Goldstone was an all-around athlete without peer, a four-year standout in football, basketball and baseball, a member of the National Honor Society. He was also modest, straight arrow and unfailingly polite.

As a rangy end, Ed caught touchdown passes for Amity football teams that lost just one game in two years; he even stepped in as quarterback when an appendectomy sidelined the incumbent. On the basketball court, he averaged 25 points per game as a senior and accumulated more than 1,500 points across four seasons and was selected to two All-State teams. He was twice a District League all-star shortstop in baseball, batted in the .400 range and once hit three home runs in a game. New Haven sportswriters called him "a coach's delight" and wrote glowingly of his nice-guy qualities.

Woodbridge address notwithstanding, Goldstone is quick to dispel the image of money in his background. Financially, at least, he was not a golden boy. "I grew up in the projects of New Haven," he states. "There were hundreds of kids, an integrated setting, tightknit family, the whole bit. When I was nine or so, my family bought a modest home in the Flats section of Woodbridge. It cost $18,000."

Ed Goldstone, from Woodbridge, was a versatile scorer and rebounder for Yale in the mid-1960s. *Courtesy of Yale University Sports Information.*

When Goldstone elected to remain close to home and attend Yale, Eli partisans were understandably elated. (Harvard was his second choice.) Nor did he disappoint anyone, except perhaps the Yale football coaching staff. In concession to academics, football was deleted from his athletic repertoire at this stage; basketball and baseball (in which he was regarded as a pro prospect) became paramount.

Let's put the period in perspective. In the mid-1960s, a good Ivy League team such as Yale could compete on an equal footing with most teams across the country. With the six-four Goldstone dividing his time between forward and center, the Elis dispatched Connecticut, Fordham, Holy Cross, Massachusetts and other top squads in the East. Twice, in 1967 and '68, they challenged for the Ivy League title, although they were unable to dislodge perennial power Princeton.

Goldstone, who had attained his full height in middle school, was a consistent double-figure scorer across three varsity seasons, averaging 14.3

points per game. As a junior, he established a still-standing Yale record with a .600 field goal percentage. "I was selective," he says with a grin.

As senior captain, Ed led Coach Joe Vancisin's team to a pair of noteworthy intersectional triumphs: a victory over Virginia in the championship game of a holiday tournament, and a 79–78 verdict over Georgia Tech, decided by a Goldstone twenty-foot jump shot with just seconds to play.

Vancisin's counterpart in baseball, Ethan Allen, regarded Goldstone "as one of the best players I ever coached." In three seasons as the Elis' varsity third baseman, Ed batted a composite .330 and walloped 13 home runs, highlighted by a school-record eight as a senior. He was selected as the team's Most Valuable Player as a junior and senior. The Goldstone leadership qualities were evident on the diamond, too: he captained the Yale squad as a senior.

The Philadelphia Phillies were impressed enough to draft Goldstone following his graduation from Yale (BA in American studies) in 1968 and three months after his marriage to Marris Rosen. (They have two children, Mathew, twenty-one, and Daniel, eighteen). But his professional baseball career fizzled after three seasons. As Ed recalls: "You hear the term 'big league power.' I played with Greg Luzinski in Huron, South Dakota. The guy could hit line drives over the center-field wall. It was exciting. I never saw a guy hit the ball that hard."

Now an angular 185-pounder, Edward Goldstone limits his athletic endeavors to jogging these days. "Fifteen years of jogging evaporated my upper body," he says.

Not Paradise

Warren Harding High School is an oasis of hope amid urban blight, but it is far from Camelot. There are thugs among the student body of one thousand; sometimes there are "disturbances," such as the recent Christmas assembly when a teacher was injured while attempting to break up a fight. Drug dealers operate with impunity not far from Harding's walls. Shootings are commonplace on neighborhood streets.

"Harding is a mirror of society," says Bob Cole. "Eighty to eighty-five percent of the kids want to learn. But now the tough guys don't have switchblades, they have guns. The rough kids are rougher."

Cole speaks about one of his football players who lived in the dregs of Father Panik Village. Each night he went to bed with the sounds of gunfire echoing in his ears. "He was never so scared."

Today's students, says Anne Giroux, "are the products of their environment. They have to deal with crime and drugs and sex and poverty. They are more street-wise than book-wise."

"Consequently," she says, "the role of educators has expanded to meet the multiple needs of students who daily—quite literally—encounter life-threatening situations. This is the environment Dr. Goldstone has tackled with unflinching optimism."

Although he wasn't the initiator, Goldstone has expanded the Cluster Program for freshmen, in which three teachers are assigned to work closely with students throughout the school day. Consistent hands-on contact breeds confidence and eases a first-year student into the high school mainstream. Fewer students drop out.

Goldstone has also expanded the number of awards assemblies. Low achievers are rewarded for their accomplishments, thus receiving a much-needed boost to their self-esteem. Once encouraged, a student is apt to strive for even better results.

The principal also receives high marks for his pursuit of support from the local business community through the Adopt-A-School program and for his attendance at athletic events and other extracurricular activities. "When he started, we were awestruck that he attended every event," says Giroux. "We asked him to cut back because we didn't want him to burn out, but I don't believe he's reduced his schedule."

Bentley agrees: "He comes to most of the games. That's important to the kids."

He might be low-key and self-effacing, but Ed Goldstone's dedication and contributions are being recognized on a larger scale. On December 20, at another holiday assembly, he was presented a citation by State Representative Americo Santiago, an acknowledgment of his work on behalf of Harding's minority students.

"He's always a student advocate," says Giroux. "It was a well-deserved honor."

Fairfield County Advocate, January 23–29, 1992

New England's Finest Player Goes One-on-One

If you're searching for the finest college basketball player in New England, look no further than Tony Hanson. While most players excel in one or two facts of the game but are deficient in other areas, the University of Connecticut's senior captain combines all the skills—dribbling, shooting, rebounding, passing, running the floor. He is the one man capable of taking down a rebound under the defensive basket, dribbling the length of the court and depositing two points at the other end.

Before the current week is history, he will have scored the most points in UConn basketball history, no mean feat when you consider that Wes Bialosuknia, Art Quimby and Toby Kimball wore the blue and white uniform.

At twenty-one, Tony Hanson is an extremely aware young man, dedicated to the proposition that life is for the living. Few approach basketball—or life in general—with as much zest.

Here are Hanson's views on his career, UConn basketball, Coach Dee Rowe, his halcyon days at Holy Cross High and more.

Don Harrison: Although you're often referred to as a native of Waterbury, you were born elsewhere, weren't you?

Tony Hanson: I was born in Kingston, Jamaica. I came here when I was four.

DH: Can you remember anything about Jamaica?

TH, chuckling: Playing with toys in the field and things like that.

DH: Although you were born in Jamaica, you aren't totally Jamaican, are you?

TH: I'm a mixture, predominantly Chinese. Most of my people are oriental.

DH: Sum up, if you will, your athletic career at the university.

TH: Pending on what happens this year, I'm satisfied. I'm very happy with the way it's been going so far. We've been in a [post-season] tournament every year that I've played. I'm with a program on the rise, and I've done a big chunk of helping it get there. This year's team is young, of course. It's a pleasure to play with the people we have now; they have fine personalities and are willing to learn. Before the season is over, we're going to have some fun.

DH: What does the captaincy mean to you?

When it came to taking the ball to the basket, Tony Hanson had few equals. *Courtesy of University of Connecticut Athletic Communications.*

TH: It's an honor. I hold the position with much pride. To be among all those distinguished captains we've had here makes me feel very proud. I look on it as a challenge, to help the young people mature.

DH: Compare this year's team with the others you played on.

TH: My first two years the team was very talented as far as individual talent goes. Last season we played together more as a unit. This year is the best because it's more of an all-for-one cause. It's the closest I've seen to a family situation. It makes it all worthwhile.

DH: More and more people are beginning to believe that Tony Hanson is the finest player in New England. How do you feel about that?

TH, suppressing a laugh: I have to respect my talent as far as it goes. A lot of people might think differently; they're entitled to their opinion. They can come to a game and see for themselves. A lot of players might have a shooting touch or be a rebounder. I try to do everything.

DH: Which game stands out in your mind as your best from a personal standpoint?

TH: The George Washington win this season was a really big one. I concentrated on doing everything [35 points, 15 rebounds, 3 assists]. The physicalness of the game and the fact that it went down to the wire makes it stand out.

DH: I recall a slightly more productive game for you, at least from a scoring standpoint.

TH: I had thirty-six points against Fairfield as a sophomore. That was my best offensive game. That's still in my mind; it's such a big rivalry. And there's the added attraction because Fairfield is the school I nearly went to. They do play a good game; it was very physical down there last year. I'm just glad both games turned out the right way.

DH: You couldn't ask for more rabid fans than the people in Storrs.

TH: They express themselves very loudly. It's good to play before a crowd that's so enthusiastic. Four years ago, when I was deciding which school to attend, one of the reasons I picked UConn was because of the crowd. They're even there on snow nights.

DH: What do you think of the people who take cheap shots at Coach Rowe?

TH: People are entitled to their opinion. On a personal standpoint, I've always respected Coach Rowe—it's something that will be long lasting. Anybody who has dealt with Coach Rowe on a personal basis knows the kind of man he is. He's a great person, a great humanist. I guess people have come to expect more and more from the basketball team. They want everything right away.

DH: This year's team has suffered several narrow defeats, although it remains in contention for a berth in the ECAC New England Tournament in March. What are the prospects?

TH: We're a young team. I consider them a top contender for the next three or four years. I'm proud to be part of this beginning.

DH: Before too long, you will hold the career scoring record at a school with a rich basketball heritage. What are your thoughts about this?

TH: When I came here, the big talk was about Wes Bialosuknia. That was a decade ago when he played. It's time for a change. Just the fact that I'm approaching it and putting my name there makes me feel pretty good. I'll be glad to get it over with. I don't want to dwell on it.

DH: Does the fact that Bialosuknia set the record in a three-year career, and you will have broken it in three and a half years, diminish the accomplishment?
TH: No, not really. Bialosuknia was a great offensive machine. But while it will take me a little while longer to set the record, the type of players we're playing against today are better. If I stay healthy, I'll continue to add to it.
DH: Tony, you're probably not aware of this, but while you will have appeared in more games than Bialosuknia, you actually will have taken fewer shots.
TH: That's interesting. I didn't know that.
DH: Tell me about your experiences in the Olympic trials.
TH: I feel I came close to making the team. We played two or three games every night. I believe about fifty-one, fifty-two [players] were there. I played well against Quinn Buckner, especially because I got to know him so well. He's such a great player; he made me play better. I also played well against Tate Armstrong. I was a little surprised at the actual picking of the team; there was a lot of politicking involved. It gave me good exposure for a pro career, being down there with the big-time names.
DH: Then the pros are interested?
TH: I know some of them have been there at a lot of games. There's been no formal contact, but Boston, especially Red Auerbach. And the New York Knicks. I'm not even concerned right now. I'm going to concentrate on the rest of my college career first.
DH: Do you have a steady young lady?
TH: No. You might say I deal with priorities. An intimate relationship tends to be a lot of work. The things I'm concerned about now are basketball and my studies.
DH: You're doing well in your studies?
TH: Yes. I'll graduate on time. I'll have my degree in special education.
DH: Along that line, you've worked at the Mansfield Training School a number of times, haven't you?
TH: The past three summers. The types of kids I've worked with have given me good exposure for the type of degree I will have. Mansfield has made me see a lot of life we take for granted as so-called normal people. I wish it could be exposed to the young people so they can help. It's given me the sense of being so sure in my thoughts. TV only gives you a brief outlook on it. They're beautiful people, like me and you. They just need a little more help. Just to see them smile and laugh. Too long we've shunned them, pretend they don't exist.

DH: I can't recall whether it was you or Gary Franks who did not have an abundance of basketball ability as a youngster.

TH: Gary always had ability. I think that story would apply to me. There were so many great players at Driggs. I would work hard at it.

DH: Things got better for you when you entered Holy Cross.

TH: Going to Holy Cross made it an actualization, under the leadership of Coach Tim McDonald. Before then, it was just Gary. Nobody knew me as Tony. Who the hell is Tony? I remember when all my buddies were there for a game with Wilby, Larry Chapman was on me. Coach [Jack] Delaney told him to check Tony Hanson, and he said, "No, I'm checking Gary."

Hanson acknowledges applause from the crowd after receiving an award from UConn Director of Athletics Jeff Hathaway at halftime of the Huskies' 2007 game against South Florida in Hartford. At right is Dee Rowe, who coached Hanson at UConn. *Steven Valenti / Courtesy of Waterbury Republican-American.*

DH: And then there was the 20-0 regular season when you were a senior.

TH: I think it instilled the winning attitude I've tried to portray up here. We were 2-18 in my sophomore year, and then we turned it around. I've seen it from both perspectives.

DH: That was a superior team, wasn't it?

TH: I would have to admit that except for the Wilbur Cross teams, I haven't seen a better one. The biggest victory was the one over Hartford Public, but ending the season 20-0 made it so special. It hadn't been done before, or in a long time.

DH: Who was it that beat you in the state quarterfinals?

TH: Fitch of Groton. They had two really good ballplayers, George... I've forgotten his name and Darrell Henderson. But if we hadn't lost Mark Duquette, a fantastic high school player, with a broken wrist, I really think we would have gone all the way.

DH: What happens if pro basketball isn't for you?

TH: I'd have a few alternatives. I could go for my master's on an administrative level. A lot of opportunities will be open for me.

DH: What does Waterbury, the city and its people, mean to you?

TH: I could never forget the city. If I could do a little something for it…I hold it in high esteem.

Waterbury Sunday Republican, January 16, 1977

LUCKETT'S HOMECOMING

Walter Luckett was born and raised in Bridgeport, which is just a quick dribble away from Fairfield University, but he could have been three thousand miles away from home Monday night.

If the Stags rolled out the red carpet, it was exclusively for themselves, as they made Luckett and his Ohio University teammates feel about as welcome as a Republican in John Bailey's living room. Luckett might be the nation's fourteenth-leading scorer, but Fairfield's Ray Kelly limited him to 15 points—8 under his per-game average. Ohio U might be in first place in the Mid-American Conference, but the Stags raced to a 37–12 lead and won going away. The final score, 91–80, gave no indication of the game's one-sidedness.

All in all, it was no way to treat a native son playing his first—and only—game in the Northeast this year. But if Walter Everett Luckett was a disconsolate young man Monday evening, he was a laughing, smiling carefree twenty-year-old for most of the weekend.

Ohio U's visit to Fairfield gave the Bobcats' six-five sophomore the opportunity to visit his parents, Mr. and Mrs. Walter Luckett Sr., and his three brothers: Darrell, sixteen; Larry, thirteen; and Norman, eleven. "Darrell is a guard, a set-up guard, at Kolbe," Walt noted. On Sunday evening, Joan Luckett prepared a scrumptious dinner for the oldest, and most famous, member of the Luckett clan and some of his teammates.

It was good to be home with his family, in the city in which he built a national reputation in high school. First-team scholastic All-American at Kolbe. New England's all-time scoring leader with 2,691 points, a 39-point scoring average as a senior, a 31.4 scoring average for his high school career, a personal high of 58 points against Stratford High. And, remarkably, one of just three scholastic players to have his jersey placed in the Naismith Memorial Basketball Hall of Fame.

Why did Bridgeport's most famous native son go so far afield to further his education and basketball career? Why didn't he stay closer to home? "I liked the school. It's in a nice college town [Athens, Ohio], and they have a good business school," Luckett said.

He also likes the Bobcats' coach, a bespectacled fifty-four-year-old gentleman named Jim Snyder, and the fact that Ohio University plays its home games in the 13,080-seat Convocation Center.

"I thought about staying closer to home," Walt said. "I knew about Fairfield. Fred

Walter Luckett scores in traffic for Ohio University. *Courtesy of Ohio University Sports Information.*

Barakat is a good friend of mine. I didn't have much interest in UConn."

If Connecticut basketball fans in particular and New England fans in general are disappointed in Luckett's choice of colleges, he isn't. He's thriving at Ohio U. He is, at six-five and 207 pounds, one inch taller and some 20 pounds heavier than the figures on the school roster. Snyder, who is completing his twenty-fifth season as the Bobcats' coach, prefers to employ Luckett at guard, the position he will play as a pro.

Walt has already broken two Ohio University scoring records this season, with 522 points and 217 field goals, and if he can maintain his 22.7 scoring average, Ken Kowall's 20.9 norm, set in 1970–71, will become another former record.

A gifted left-handed shooter whose range is twenty-five feet and beyond, Luckett has connected on nearly 49 percent of his field goal attempts and 72 percent of his free throws thus far. Indicative of improvements in other facets of his game are his 63 assists, which trail team leader Larry Slappy by four.

Walter Luckett is a contented young man at the moment, much happier than he was last season, when knee problems necessitated surgery and some on-court problems—he averaged *only* 13.5 points—caused some people to wonder about certain overrated basketball players. The price of fame—he was, after all, *Sports Illustrated*'s cover boy ever before taking his first shot as a collegian—seemed too high.

Now that his life is in order, now that things are falling into place, this question remains: will he complete his four years of education at Ohio U, or will the lure of professional basketball prove too enticing?

"That's a difficult question," he chuckled. "It depends…if they [the pros] are going to give me a little bit of money, I'll stay. I want to stay. If we win the conference and go to the NCAA Tournament, we'll get a lot of publicity."

A lot would seem to depend on Walt's fiancée, Valita Holley, a Bridgeport girl who attends Brown University. Their wedding is tentatively scheduled for sometime during, or just after, Walt's senior year. This special date could dictate Luckett's basketball future.

Waterbury Republican, February 20, 1974

MATTHEWS COURTS NBA JOB

A dozen youngsters watch intently as Wes Matthews lofts foul shots with an undersized basketball. On the periphery, several adults follow the action with casual interest. Matthews deposits nine straight attempts before missing, hits another, misses again and then starts another streak. The youngsters' gaze remains fixed.

On this Saturday in November, Wes Matthews demonstrates his foul-shooting prowess on Pop-A-Shot, a new indoor basketball game equipped with an electronic scoreboard and timer. The scene is at the Arctic Sports Shop on East Main Street, where Matthews worked when he was a student at Warren Harding High School. "He was the best Converse salesman we ever had," chuckles Perry Pilotti, the store's founder and genial goodwill ambassador.

Wes flashes a broad smile at Pilotti's remark. "You got a sneaker contract from Converse years later, didn't you?" Perry says. Another smile.

Wes Matthews with the Atlanta Hawks in the early 1980s. *Courtesy of Jim Kish.*

At the moment, Wesley Joel Matthews is out of work. His appearance at Arctic is a mere cameo. After two seasons as a reserve guard with the Los Angeles Lakers, after contributing to back-to-back NBA championships with the team of Magic and Kareem and James Worthy, after eight NBA seasons in all, Wes is seeking employment.

"I'm negotiating with a few teams," he explains. "We've talked with Houston and Miami, both expansion teams. New Jersey would be nice; I would like to play close to home."

At twenty-nine, the former Harding and University of Wisconsin star believes he has "five or six" seasons of high-caliber play in front of him. But where? "I'm still optimistic about it," he says. "There's a team out there that needs a quality guard."

What happened with the Lakers?

Easy answer. When the club selected Notre Dame's All-American, David Rivers, on the first round of the 1988 NBA draft, the Laker backcourt became overpopulated with point guards. Magic Johnson (arguably the game's best), Matthews and Rivers. Wes was deemed expendable.

Hey, thanks for the memories. Wes Matthews has no regrets.

His two seasons with the Lakers, albeit in a backup role, represent the high point of his well-traveled NBA stay. (Washington, Atlanta, Philadelphia, Chicago and San Antonio were other stops.) Two years with two of the finest teams in the history of professional basketball, two years of playing in front of Jack Nicholson and 17,504 others at the Forum, teaming up with some of the game's all-time stars.

"It was a great experience, the championships, the ticker-tape parade after last season. I take my hat off to [General Manager] Jerry West for letting me play," Matthews says.

"Starting out here, going to the Boys Club, the Shehan Center, Harding and then getting the opportunity to play with the Lakers, well, that was great."

He will miss his friendship with Kareem Abdul-Jabbar, the seven-two center who, at age forty-one, continues to loft sky hooks against men nearly twenty years his junior. "I admired him as a kid, and I'll miss being with him on his last farewell around the league. I sat next to him on all the team flights."

He'll miss, too, the opportunities to contribute to Laker victories, such as the occasion last year when "due to [Michael] Cooper's absence," he scored "sixteen or seventeen points" in a nationally televised game against the Detroit Pistons.

Matthews was a two-time All-Stater at Warren Harding High. *Courtesy of Jim Kish.*

In one respect, Wes Matthews was the vanguard, the first of three Harding graduates to reach the NBA as a first-round draft choice. Within a nine-year span, it was Matthews (1980, Washington Bullets), John Bagley (1982, Cleveland Cavaliers) and Charles Smith (1988, Philadelphia 76ers).

On the other hand, he was "the cocky kid" who followed Frank Oleynick, Walter Luckett and Barry McLeod, Bridgeport's talented triumvirate of the early 1970s. Luckett, who lofted feathery jump shots for Kolbe High School, and Oleynick and McLeod, first cousins who played the game with flair at Notre Dame High.

Either way, Matthews's place is secure as a player who helped to establish the Park City as the citadel of high school basketball, the number one hotbed in the sport.

"When I started, it was always New Haven. The Hillhouses and Crosses always overpowered us," Wes recalls. "We had a small team and had to rely on running. Finally, we had a showdown in New Haven, and Harding came out on top. Now, the younger generation follows us, respects us."

"He had extraordinary gifts," remembers Jim Kish, who was Matthews's coach at Harding. "He only had a marginal outside shot but was an excellent shooter in the transition game, extremely quick and a leaper's leaper. He reminded me of Norm Nixon, a super-quick point guard."

As a high school senior, Matthews averaged a sublime 30.5 points (including a high of 58) and was a unanimous Most Valuable Player selection in the prestigious Dapper Dan Classic in Pittsburgh. One national all-star team placed Wes on its first five with Magic Johnson, Jeff Ruland, Albert King and Gene Banks.

"I attribute a lot of the success I had to great coaching," Wes says. "Jim Kish at Harding and Sandy Sulzycki at Orcutt Boys Club. They realized our [running] style; they didn't try to restrict our game."

Wes Matthews was seven months old when his family moved to Bridgeport from Sarasota, Florida. For him, the Port has always represented home (although Los Angeles is his current residence). While he waits for the NBA to call, he's spending some time with his mother, Mrs. Ethel Matthews, and other family members and contacting old friends. "I'm working out at the Y, constantly staying in shape."

His mother, a pleasant woman who has been active in community work, is emphatic in her desire to see the third of her four children return to the NBA. "He's got me where I'm pumped up and positive. I'm praying and hoping he'll be back playing ball," she says.

Should the NBA door be closed, what then? Wes talks about coaching, about "giving back to the game." But he also voices a concern for Bridgeport and its young people, about contributing something to today's legion of jump shooters.

"Anything I can do to help, telling kids to say 'no' to drugs, doing things like that," he says. "I've been on every side of town. Father Panik Village, P.T. We used to hang out at the Lafayette Mall because that was the thing to do.

"They should reopen the Boys Club, have something for [today's kids] to do. Give them a dream about being a basketball player, a baseball player. Being a doctor."

Wes Matthews's own dream remains the same; it bears the initials N-B-A. "Your dream can happen," he says. "It's just a matter of sticking with your dream."

Bridgeport Light, November 30, 1988

FROM NORWALK TO NIAGARA TO BASKETBALL'S TOP HONOR

Inch for inch and pound for pound, there may not have been a greater basketball player than Calvin Murphy. At only five-nine and about 165 pounds, he was capable of outscoring the Goliaths wherever he played—at Norwalk High School, Niagara University and with the Houston Rockets.

In a twenty-season career encompassing high school, college and the pros, he generated an astounding number of points, 23,616, and was accorded accolades ranging from high school All-America to major college All-America to National Basketball Association All-Star.

Calvin Jerome Murphy was the first of a breed, a small man excelling in a big man's game. And now he has reached the pinnacle in his sport: election to the Naismith Memorial Basketball Hall of Fame. On May 10—one day after his forty-fifth birthday—the Norwalk native will be inducted with Julius Erving, Bill Walton, Dan Issel, Walt Bellamy, Dick McGuire, the Olympic star Ann Meyers and the Russian Olympian Juliana Semenova in ceremonies at Springfield, Massachusetts.

"I've finally achieved something that puts everything in perspective," said a trim and graying Murphy, who now lives in the Houston area and works for the Rockets as an analyst for home and away telecasts and handles community relations. "This is the ultimate," he said. "Everything's about timing, and this was my time."

Going into the Hall of Fame "is beyond my wildest dreams," said Murphy, who as a teenager only dreamed of starting for his high school team.

In a different time, basketball was viewed as a sport for giants; "small" men were six-footers,

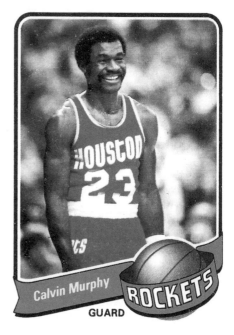

Calvin Murphy, 1979 Topps card. *Courtesy of Frank Corr.*

72

and those of lesser stature were ignored. Dave Bike, who played against Murphy in Connecticut's state high school tournament and at the Biddy League level, was among the doubters.

"I thought there was a question: was he too small to play in college even before the NBA," remembered Bike, now the head coach at Sacred Heart University. "You couldn't guard him one-on-one, but you had to wonder about his size," Bike said. "What he's done has to be regarded as one of the greater accomplishments of sports."

Alvin Clinkscales, who was Bike's coach at Notre Dame of Bridgeport when Murphy was playing for Norwalk, has a vivid

Calvin Murphy of Norwalk High drives for two points. *Courtesy of Norwalk Museum.*

recollection of the Lancers' game against Norwalk in the semifinals of the 1965 Class L state tournament. "We were great on defense; we had all kinds of presses," he recalled. "I told our team we were going to give Calvin his thirty-five and shut down the rest of his team and we'd win.

"Well, Calvin got his thirty-five, and we won by a little," Clinkscales said. "After the game, I went over to Calvin and told him, 'You were the best ever against our press.' Very innocently, he asked, 'What press?'"

To most observers, Calvin Murphy remains the greatest high school player to come out of Connecticut, regarded as superior to "Super John" Williamson from Wilbur Cross in New Haven and Walter Luckett of Kolbe in Bridgeport.

Murphy's scoring feats at Norwalk bordered on the surreal, especially his state-record 40.4 scoring average as a senior in the 1965–66 season and career average of 32.2. His career-high scholastic total of 62 points was recorded in a victory over Roger Ludlowe of Fairfield on January 14, 1966.

During his final two high school seasons, the Bears assembled a 44-4 record, culminating with the 1966 Class L state championship.

"A Perfect Gentleman"

"He was the greatest player for his size and a perfect gentleman as well," recalled Ralph King, now the athletic director at cross-town rival Brien McMahon High and the Senators' head coach during the Murphy era.

"I had just come to town, and the first time I saw Calvin Murphy he was following a moving vehicle in the Memorial Day parade," King said. "There was a basket on the back, and he was shooting. He must have been ten, eleven years old."

A slighter older Calvin Murphy had another role in that parade. The exceptional hand-eye coordination that enabled him to excel on the basketball court was put to use with a baton. "He used to lead the Norwalk High School band in the parade," said his mother, Ina Miller. "He learned to twirl a baton from my sister, Alfrida. He even twirled in competition at the New York World's Fair."

Invariably, Murphy's scoring exploits put the intra-city games in the Norwalk win column, but King still savors the night McMahon prevailed. "The only loss in Murphy's senior year was to McMahon by a score of something like 67–61," he said. "The gym in the old Norwalk High was so crowded, I had to stand behind our bench."

All-American Calvin Murphy is too much for two Providence defenders. *Courtesy of Niagara University Athletic Communications.*

74

An All-American and two-time All-State selection at Norwalk, Murphy solidified his status by earning the Most Valuable Player award in the post-season Dapper Dan Classic in Pittsburgh. He merely scored thirty-seven points.

At Niagara, the jet-quick guard was an instant sensation, averaging a remarkable 48.9 points with the Purple Eagles' freshman team. Fans who witnessed his magic would leave the gym before the varsity game to join Murphy in the Student Union, where he would regale his audience.

Murphy accumulated a prodigious number of points with the Niagara varsity—2,548 in three All-America seasons. His career scoring average of 33.1 still ranks as the fourth highest in National Collegiate Athletic Association annals, behind Pete Maravich of Louisiana State (44.2), Austin Carr of Notre Dame (34.6) and Oscar Robertson of Cincinnati (33.8).

In the third game of his junior year, Murphy earned nationwide headlines when he registered 68 points against Syracuse on December 7, 1968—still the third-highest total against an NCAA Division I opponent. Niagara won, 118–110.

Largest Crowd for College Game

As a collegian, he made two appearances in his home state, both against Fairfield University in the old New Haven Arena. For the first meeting on January 27, 1968, the aging building was jammed to its 5,100 capacity—which represented the largest crowd to view a college game in Connecticut.

On that night, a supporting player—Larry Cirina, a Fairfield senior guard who would average only 11.7 points that season—upstaged college basketball's leading man by outscoring Calvin Murphy, 33–28. The Stags prevailed over the Purple Eagles, 88–85.

With considerably less fanfare, Murphy generated a comparatively quiet 25 points two years later when Niagara defeated Fairfield, 71–65, in New Haven before 4,500 fans.

The 1969–70 season was the most satisfying of his years in a Purple Eagle uniform. With Frank Layden taking over as coach, Niagara shook off the stigma of 12-12 and 11-13 seasons by assembling a 22-7 record and earned a berth in the NCAA Tournament.

Murphy capitalized on his fame in the spring of 1970 by leading the "Calvin Murphy All-Stars" on a tour of Connecticut. He scored 89 points in an exhibition game at Kennedy High School in Waterbury, 90 points someplace else and 105 points in Rockville.

Despite his small size, Calvin Murphy was a standout from the outset in the National Basketball Association. Drafted by the Rockets when they were based in San Diego, he finished fourth in the 1971 Rookie-of-the-Year balloting and was chosen to the league's All-Rookie team. In 1979, he played in the NBA All-Star Game.

For eleven straight seasons, Murphy scored one thousand or more points with the Rockets and, along with Rick Barry, helped to elevate free-throw accuracy to a new plateau. He established a record with a .958 percentage (206-215) in 1980–81, which was the same season he sank seventy-eight consecutive free throws—a league record that was tied this month by Mark Price of the Cleveland Cavaliers. Murphy's thirteen-year scoring average of 17.9 is the fifteenth highest among those playing in at least one thousand NBA games.

Norwalk youngsters of today are familiar with Calvin Murphy's basketball accomplishments. The two players who make up Norwalk High's current backcourt, George Alexander and Don Sikorski, honed their skills in the Calvin Murphy League, and they have studied the jerseys, autographed balls and other memorabilia in the school's trophy case.

"I know he was a real great player, for his size one of the best or *the* best," Sikorski said. "I saw him play in a charity game once; he could still shoot. We were excited to see him at our game and show his support."

On February 9, the day after his election to the Basketball Hall of Fame was announced, Calvin Murphy returned to his hometown to watch the Norwalk-McMahon game. He beamed and waved and tossed up the ceremonial opening jump ball. "I don't see too many high school games except for my hometown," he said with a smile. "And I want Norwalk to win."

Perhaps inspired by his presence, the Bears went out and throttled the team coached by Murphy's brother, Bob Miller, 63–48. "It meant a lot having him here," Alexander said. "It showed he didn't forget where he came from."

New York Times, April 11, 1993

The Players

Murphy by the Numbers

HONORS
Elected to Naismith Memorial Basketball Hall of Fame, 1993
Elected to National Collegiate Basketball Hall of Fame, 2006
SINGLE-GAME HIGHS
Norwalk High School: 62 points v. Roger Ludlowe, 1/14/66
Niagara University: 68 points v. Syracuse, 12/7/68
Houston Rockets: 57 points (regular season) v. New Jersey, 3/18/78; 42 points (playoffs) v. San Antonio, 4/17/81

NORWALK HIGH SCHOOL, 1963–66
Parade Magazine All-American Team, 1965–66
New Haven Register All-State Team, 1964–65, 1965–66
MVP, Dapper Dan Tournament, Pittsburgh, 1966
All-FCIAC, 1963–64, 1964–65, 1965–66
Led Norwalk to the Class L state championship in 1965–66
Leading scorer in Connecticut, 1964–65 (31.7), 1965–66 (40.4)
Set state scoring record with 40.4 average, 1965–66

NIAGARA UNIVERSITY, 1967–70
First-team consensus All-America, 1968–69, 1969–70
Second-team consensus All-America, 1967–68
Inducted into Niagara Hall of Fame, 1975
His career scoring average of 33.1 ranks fourth among Division I players
His 68-point game against Syracuse is the third highest against a Division I opponent
Scored 30 or more points in 42 of 77 varsity games
Averaged 48.9 points on Niagara freshman team, 1966–67

SAN DIEGO/HOUSTON ROCKETS, 1970–83
NBA All-Star, 1978–79
NBA All-Rookie Team, 1970–71
Number 23 retired, 3/17/84
Second-highest free throw percentage in an NBA season, .958 (206-215)
Third-highest free throw percentage in NBA history, .892 (3445-3864)
Second-highest free throw percentage in NBA playoff history, .932 (165-177)
Set NBA record (since broken) with 78 consecutive free throws made, 12/27/80–2/20/81
Scored a Rockets record 57 points against New Jersey, 3/18/78
Ranks first in Rockets history in assists (4,402); second in points (17,949), games (1,002), steals (1,165), field goals (7,247), free throws (3,445) and free throw percentage (.892); tenth in scoring average (17.9)

YEAR BY YEAR

Norwalk High School

Years	G	Pts.	Avg.
1963–64	18	460	25.6
1964–65	24	761	31.7
1965–66	24	969	40.4
Totals	**66**	**2190**	**33.2**

Niagara University

Years	G	Pts.	Avg.
1967–68	24	916	38.2
1968–69	24	778	32.4
1969–70	29	854	29.4
Totals	**77**	**2548**	**33.1**

San Diego/Houston Rockets

Years	G	Pts.	Avg.
1970–71	82	1298	15.8
1971–72	82	1491	18.2
1972–73	77	1001	13.0
1973–74	81	1652	20.4
1974–75	78	1455	18.7
1965–76	82	1722	21.0
1976–77	82	1464	17.9
1977–78	76	1949	25.6
1978–79	82	1660	20.2
1979–80	76	1520	20.0
1980–81	76	1266	16.7
1981–82	64	655	10.2
1982–83	64	816	12.8
Totals	**1002**	**17949**	**17.9**

NBA Playoffs

Years	G	Pts.	Avg.
1974–75	8	195	24.4
1976–77	12	232	19.3
1978–79	2	26	13.0
1979–80	7	131	18.7
1980–81	19	344	18.1
1981–82	3	17	5.7
Totals	**51**	**945**	**18.5**

A TRUE LEADER ON THE COURT, A FRIEND OFF IT

Conducting research online is an accepted practice these days for students, educators, journalists and just about everyone else. But sometimes the revelations can be jarring.

Such was the case for me on a recent evening when I typed in "Ralph Paolillo basketball" and the first response on my screen was his obituary. Cancer, the text said, had ended the life of this warm, outgoing person at age seventy on January 21, 2010. I was both stunned and saddened by the news and, at the same time, reminded of my own mortality.

Ralph and I had gone through school together, from the fourth grade in the old Union School all the way through East Haven High School. We even shared homeroom 306, where Mr. Levy—a bespectacled mathematics teacher who bore a resemblance to Superman's alter ego, Clark Kent—reigned.

Ralph A. Paolillo Jr. was an immensely likeable person, truly a friend to all. Thumb through the pages of the school's 1957 *Pioneer* yearbook and one will discover he was voted Most Popular, Best Mixer, Best All-Around, Nicest Smile and, not surprisingly, Most Athletic.

Although standing just five-ten, he could play basketball better than most and shares the distinction with Tony Massari '54 as being the only East Haven players to earn All-State recognition two straight years.

"Ralph was one of my boys during our golden years, when we never lost a ballgame," remembered Frank Crisafi, now eighty-seven, who coached the Easties to six state titles during a remarkable thirty-three-year career. "He was a leader in every sense of the word. He played the game with his head; he really worked at it. He had a great, great jump shot from outside the arc. Ralphie and Tony were my two best shooters."

East Haven won seventy-seven consecutive games during our first three years in high school, a state record that would endure for more than two decades, until a Corny Thompson–led Middletown High team exceeded that number in 1978.

The Easties' streak ended in memorable fashion, in the championship game of the 1956 Class M state tournament, when Stonington—led by six-seven Wayne Lawrence—prevailed by a 62–60 score in Yale's Payne

Ralph Paolillo, a two-time All-Stater at East Haven High, went on to a fine career at St. Anselm. *Courtesy of St. Anselm College Sports Information.*

Whitney Gymnasium. (Lawrence went on to a fine playing career at Texas A&M and was the Boston Celtics' fifth-round draft choice in 1960.)

Paolillo was a junior in 1956 yet earned a place on the *Register*'s All-State team. He would repeat in 1957, when he, as team captain, and fellow All-Stater John DeCaprio lifted the Yellow Jackets to a 19-3 record and the school's third state Class M title in four years.

When he was a senior, Paolillo's scoring average soared to 20.0, and he was at his best in the state tournament. With Ralph pouring in 26 points, the Easties avenged the previous year's loss to Stonington with a 76–52 verdict in the semifinals. Then he followed up with 16 points as the Yellow Jackets upended Seymour, 57–38, in the championship game. Not surprisingly, he was awarded the Warren Sampson Memorial Trophy as the tournament's Most Valuable Player.

Vin Murray, the Shelton coach, declared that Ralph "steadied the team when the pressure was on. He has a shooting eye second to none."

Paolillo earned a basketball scholarship to Saint Anselm College, then, as now, one of the most respected small-college programs in the Northeast. For three seasons, he was a double-figure scorer for the Hawks, reaching a peak of 15.1 points per game as a junior. Twice, his teams advanced to the NCAA Tournament.

What caused his scoring average to dip to 4.8 as a senior? "Ralph had injured his foot at a summertime job in New Haven harbor and needed about one hundred stitches," recalled his younger brother, Anthony. "He was afraid he was going to lose his scholarship, but he came back and played pretty well."

After earning a bachelor's degree in 1962, Ralph Paolillo continued to play the game well with semipro teams, notably the Columbus Bears and New Haven Airways. He spent the last twenty-seven years of his professional life as director of community development for the City of West Haven.

In 1989, Ralph was among the third group of four elected to East Haven High School's Alumni Association Hall of Fame. Several years later, he was selected as one of the all-time top twenty-five high school players in Greater New Haven—a rich and well-deserved honor.

"I was always very proud," said Crisafi, "to say Ralph was one of mine."

New Haven Register, February 12, 2010

CHARLES ISN'T JUST ANOTHER SMITH

Six Smiths appear in the *1988–89 Official NBA Register* published by the *Sporting News*. There is Larry, the Golden State forward, and Kenny, the Sacramento guard; Derek, the Sacramento forward; Keith, the Milwaukee guard; and Otis, a swingman most recently with Golden State. On page 261, listed among the rookies is the Smith we care most about: Charles of the Los Angeles Clippers.

Charles Daniel Smith. Performing on a team that lost three times as often as it won, the six-ten forward distinguished himself as a National Basketball Association rookie this past season. His scoring average was a bright 16.3 (with a high of 34 points). His rebound average was a decent 6.5.

If the Clippers won less often than their followers would have liked, Smith at least provided some solace. When a more-publicized rookie named Danny Manning went down with a knee injury in early January, Charles was forced to turn up his game a notch. He did. The team finished 21-61, but Smith was selected to the NBA's All-Rookie Team.

"I didn't play as well as I could have," he admits with candor. "But the way the last month went, I wish the season could have gone on longer. I

Charles Smith in action with the Los Angeles Clippers. *Courtesy of Wilson Sporting Goods.*

adjusted well later in the season, but I was playing the three, four and five positions and never was stable. Everything was confusing for a lot of the season, but we came together and played well at the end."

Charles Smith was home for a while last month, his first extended visit to his native Bridgeport in three years. He played some hoops with friends, spent some time with his mother, Dorothy Lee, and made an appearance on behalf of Wilson Sporting Goods at Arctic Sports Shop. He's endorsing a sneaker, appropriately named Hang Time, for Wilson.

If my calculations are correct, Smith is the fifth man from the Park City to play major league basketball in this decade. Wes Matthews and John Bagley, both also from Warren Harding; John Garris from Bassick; and Frank Oleynick from Notre Dame preceded him. (If he had hired a more competent agent, Kolbe's Walter Luckett might have joined this list, but that's another story.) At six-ten, Charles is not only the tallest but the best compensated of the group.

As the third player chosen in the June 1988 NBA draft, he was able to secure a multi-year, multimillion-dollar contract with the Clippers. Life is sweet…and becoming sweeter. There is a home in Marina del Ray, the relationship with Wilson, marketing arrangements for T-shirts and sweatshirts, a basketball camp this summer in Pittsburgh. There's even some talk of his performing in a movie.

Charles Smith might be on the fast track, but it's nice to be able to catch your breath once in a while. One should take time to reflect, to remember those who helped along the way. Above all, Charles remembers Coach Charlie Bentley at Harding High. "People don't realize my first year of high school I got very good grades," he explains. "Next year I kind of slacked off. Coach Bentley, he stressed that I get my grades up. With support from my mother, I got a 3.4 my last semester. I learned a lot being at Harding."

Education was an important part of Smith's life at Harding, more important than contributing jump shots and rebounds to the first two of the Presidents' five consecutive Class L state championships. It remained a high priority at the University of Pittsburgh, too, where he established career scoring (2,045) and shot-blocking (346) records and attained All-American status.

"I'm probably the first basketball player there to get his degree on time in the last couple of years," Smith says with pardonable pride. The BA was obtained in liberal studies, with an emphasis on communications. Charles Smith is as well spoken as he is elongated; one can envision him years hence providing expert commentary on NBA telecasts, or perhaps portraying an urbane detective a la Sidney Poitier.

Between the last of his Big East seasons at Pitt and the first of his NBA seasons in the City of the Angels was the Olympic season in Seoul, South Korea. Charles Smith has mixed emotions about his experiences last summer with the U.S. Olympic basketball team.

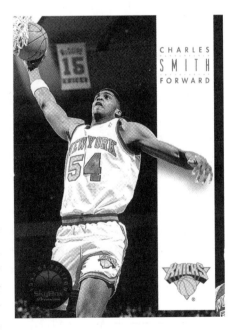

"A major disappointment," he says of the Americans' loss to the Soviet Union in the semifinals of the Olympic tournament and ultimate bronze medal finish. "We should have won; there's no excuse for the loss. We played one bad game."

Coach John Thompson employed Smith in a starting role on some occasions, as a "sixth or seventh man" at other times. Charles recalls reaching a high of "nineteen or twenty points" in one game. Despite the disappointing loss, he will cherish

Charles Smith, 1994 SkyBox card. *Courtesy of Frank Corr.*

the memories—even those associated with having only a few free days between Seoul and reporting to the Clippers' training camp.

The adjustment from college to the professional ranks and playing for one of the league's lowly teams? No problem. Well, a few problems.

"The big difference is the length of schedule, eighty-two games, and the travel," he says. "But I love the game more so now than in college. There's more freedom. Shooting the twenty-footer. Taking the ball coast to coast. Danny Manning and a lot of the other guys on the team are great."

The Clipper fans, he says, were there in abundance, despite the seemingly endless succession of defeats. "We averaged eleven thousand at home; we have our fan support. The fans who were there all the time knew what was happening with the injuries and the coaching changes."

Charles Smith is scheduled to begin a weight-training program this month in Los Angeles. A bout with the flu and strep throat in January, compounded by a sprained knee, took their toll on his 230-pound body. He dropped 12 pounds.

"I've got to get as strong as possible, be in tiptop shape when the season begins," he declares.

Greater strength and endurance will enable him to keep up with the Joneses—and Smiths—of the NBA.

Bridgeport Light, June 14, 1989

SMITH UNAFRAID OF SOPHOMORE JINX

The number on the University of Connecticut jersey is thirteen, so right away you know Chris Smith isn't superstitious. "Mark Jackson [of the Knicks] wears number thirteen, and he's doing fine," Chris says with a laugh.

Chris Smith is doing just fine, too, now that his freshman season is over. The Huskies' angular six-three guard experienced the inevitable growing pains, the start-up problems usually associated with a new venture. But on the whole, the former Kolbe-Cathedral scholastic All-American acquitted himself rather well as a rookie in the Big East and endeared himself to UConn's legions of followers.

Jim Calhoun, the man who coaches the Huskies, proclaimed Smith as "the best freshman guard in the conference." Which says a lot.

The Players

In fact, Chris Smith was asked to do a lot—defend the opposition's primary offensive threat, distribute the basketball, hit the three-pointer. Perhaps, some say, he was asked to do too much too soon.

Chris Smith isn't complaining, though. He knew he could make the quantum leap from high school—even the superior brand of basketball played in Bridgeport and environs—into the major college ranks. "It's a big adjustment here," he admits. "Everyone is so good. In high school, I was the man. The biggest adjustment here was I had to wait my turn."

Christopher Gerard Smith wasn't asked to wait too long. By game two, he was in the UConn starting lineup and contributed 13 points and five assists to a 75–44 rout of Yale. By game four, he was the team leader in scoring and assists (16 and eight, respectively) on the road against nationally ranked Purdue.

In all, Smith started seventeen of twenty-nine games in which he appeared—including the final thirteen. He averaged 11.6 points through the last sixteen games and 9.9 overall. He also finished with 87 assists, second on the squad to Tate George's 152, and committed just 40 turnovers.

One cannot quarrel with this productivity from a freshman, especially a young man who was asked to share the backcourt with a junior (George) and a senior co-captain, Phil Gamble, in arguably the nation's finest conference.

Defensively, the eighteen-year-old Bridgeport native (he turns nineteen on May 17) did a number on players with national reputations. Dana Barros? In two games, Smith limited the Boston College marksman to 7-for-27 shooting. Gerard Greene? In one of their three meetings, the Seton Hall star seemed to be wearing Smith's jersey for the evening and was able to launch only two shots, finishing with two points. And then there was the night when the quick-handed Smith blanked Georgetown's Charles Smith for some twenty-seven minutes before the Hoya All-American checked in with eight points (but only one field goal). On that occasion at least, onlookers were beginning to wonder if the correct Smith had been chosen for the U.S. Olympic team.

Chris Smith also distinguished himself on a January afternoon in the Hartford Civic Center when the Huskies wrote *fini* to their seventeen-game losing streak against St. John's. He contributed five steals, 13 points and five rebounds to UConn's cleansing 80–52 triumph. "Probably my best game," he states. "I felt very comfortable out there."

On the whole, Smith believes the Huskies' 18-13 record and quarterfinal finish in the National Invitation Tournament were satisfactory, although he contends, "There were a lot of games we could have won."

One does not reach the heights without support, without a solid foundation, and Chris knows he needn't look too far. He points to his mother, Mrs. Lola Smith, who directed him to Kolbe-Cathedral, a Catholic school that places a strong emphasis on academics and spirituality. He's also indebted to his grandmother, Mrs. Artent Smith, for her guidance.

He's appreciative of the education he received at Kolbe and of the care and concern shown by its remarkable principal, the Reverend Frank Wissel. "A great man," Smith says of Father Wissel. "So many times we'd talk in his office about college. He was there when I needed him. Kolbe definitely did a lot for me."

Chris Smith, from Bridgeport's Kolbe Cathedral High School, fires a jump shot. He accumulated a record 2,145 points during his four-year UConn career and later played three seasons with the NBA Minnesota Timberwolves. *Courtesy of University of Connecticut Athletic Communications.*

Of the three men who coached Kolbe-Cathedral during Smith's sparkling four-year career, which included a Class M state championship during his freshman season and a runner-up finish as a junior, Chris credits Rick Karpinski with "helping me the most." "We spent a lot of time together in the summer...he drove me to camps." He was, says Chris, "a friend."

Although he will be Connecticut's leading returning scorer next season, Smith's role has yet to be defined. Should George improve his shooting, he could reclaim the point guard position he lost to Chris in mid-season, thus allowing Smith to shift to off-guard and concentrate on scoring.

"We're going to be very good next year," Chris insists, "better than a lot of people think. Next year, I think you'll see six players in double digits.

"We stuck together last year, no matter if we won or lost. As I get older, I'll try to build on that tradition."

Bridgeport Light, April 26, 1989

UPDATE: Chris Smith fulfilled most of his basketball dreams. As a UConn sophomore, he was a major contributor to the 1989–90 Huskies coming within a whisker—Duke's Christian Laettner's game-winner in the East Regional finals—of advancing to the Final Four. After four seasons in Storrs, he departed with 2,145 points, still the career record. Selected by the Minnesota Timberwolves as the thirty-fourth pick in the 1992 NBA draft, he played three seasons with the club. In 2009, Chris completed the circle by returning to Kolbe Cathedral as the boys' basketball coach.

IT'LL ALWAYS BE PORKY IN BRIDGEPORT

I'll never be called anything except Frank at the University of New Haven, but I'll always be Porky in Bridgeport.
—Frank "Porky" Vieira

WEST HAVEN—By either name, he is both a legend in his own time and a legend in his own mind.

Frank Vieira, the nation's winningest college baseball coach and tenured professor. Porky Vieira, scorer of a sublime eighty-nine points in a semipro basketball game and sixty-eight points in a college game. Before that, it was little Florindo Vieira lofting long two-handed set shots for the Middle Street Boys Club's eighty-five-pounders.

For most of his fifty-five years, he has been chasing—or should it be running from?—his personal demons, as player, coach and even as workaholic college basketball referee. As Florindo, Porky, the Pork and now, for most of the past quarter century, Frank Vieira.

Athletics abound with men who are egocentric, one-dimensional and, to employ a choice Vieiraism, "a little bit of a self-centered bastard." To

Porky Vieira, poised for another productive night at Quinnipiac. *Courtesy of University of New Haven Athletics Communication.*

most of us, Frank "Porky" Vieira is a likeable egotist.

What drives this remarkable Bridgeport native? Did he always possess this fierce desire to excel, to beat the other guy's brains in? The answer: almost from the very beginning.

In the early years, his game was basketball, at the Boys Club, Central High School, Quinnipiac College, with the semipro Bridgeport Savoys, Vieira All-Stars and other semi-pro aggregations. But for the past twenty-seven years, he has been best known as the record-setting baseball coach at the University of New Haven. Last June, his Chargers came within six outs of winning the school's first NCAA Division II World Series.

"If somebody had ever mentioned that I'd be introduced at a banquet and there'd be no mention of basketball, I would have told him he was crazy," he says, grinning.

Vieira is sitting behind his desk in his small, well-appointed office near the UNH gymnasium. He is a stocky man, 5-foot-6½ and considerably heavier than when he was obliterating college scoring records in the mid-1950s. Despite middle age, the competitive fire still burns in his eyes. Behind him on the wall is a framed photograph of Steve Bedrosian, clearly the most successful of the ten former Chargers to reach baseball's Major Leagues.

"He's a class guy," Porky says of the man who won the 1987 National League Cy Young Award and who is now pitching in a World Series with the San Francisco Giants. "Bedrosian donated $5,000 to my field. He calls me when he comes to New York. 'Coach, how come you're not coming down?'"

The Players

"My field" is the Frank "Porky" Vieira Field, dedicated on December 5, 1986, to the founding coach of the UNH baseball program. In a clear display of affection for the man, some seventy former Charger players were present for the ceremony.

Vieira the baseball coach has enjoyed unparalleled success. His winning percentage of .815 leads all active coaches in Division II, far ahead of men from Florida Southern and Troy State in Alabama. With 707 total victories (against just 156 defeats), he is a strong third behind coaches at Cal Poly–Pomona and Valdosta State in Georgia. His New Haven teams have appeared in twelve College World Series—highlighted by second-place finishes in 1989 and 1980—and twenty-two post-season tournaments overall. His all-time winning percentage in the NCAA playoffs is a startling .613.

The accomplishments are impressive, but the coach professes to be unimpressed. "You're only as good as your last ballgame," he snorts. "We came within six outs of winning the national championship. I've got 707 wins. But when spring comes, I'm 0-0."

Forty-eight of his former players have signed professional contracts, a number rivaled in the Northeast only by Maine, St. John's and perhaps Seton Hall. The forty-seventh Charger to sign was Steve DiBartolomeo, the former St. Joseph High of Trumbull pitcher, who was a first-team All-American and the 1989 Division II Player of the Year. The hard-throwing DiBo is now property of the Chicago Cubs.

John Anquillare, Vieira's second in command and, in 1963, his first captain, offers the following explanation for the abundance of UNH players in the professional ranks: "Porky doesn't forget his people. He sells his kids to the pros. A lot of kids with the same ability never got the chance to play [professionally]. Our kids do."

A few years ago, Bobby Valentine of the Texas Rangers asked Vieira to join his staff as the hitting instructor. Porky considered the pluses and minuses and then declined the offer. "When I weighed it, I choked," he says. "I didn't want to do all that traveling. Now, if the Red Sox offered me the manager's chair…"

As a batting instructor, Vieira has few equals. He was a superlative outfielder in high school and in Bridgeport's Senior City League, winning three batting titles in the latter competition. He says he learned much of his coaching technique from the master, Ted Williams. "I was fortunate to spend three summers with him at his camp in Lakeville. I got to hear him every day."

In basketball, Vieira also enjoyed unrivaled success. In a game dominated by giants, the stocky guard earned All-State honors in successive seasons (1951, 1952) at Central High. As a sophomore, he was a major factor in the Hilltoppers capturing the 1950 New England scholastic championship at Boston Garden.

Lofting jump shots, hook shots and two-handed set shots from thirty feet and occasionally beyond, Porky *averaged* 32.8 points per game across four seasons at then-tiny Quinnipiac College. In the semipro ranks and facing teams of touring NBA players in exhibitions, he was apt to score 30, 40, 50 points—sometimes even more.

Why was he so obsessed with achieving excellence? An early, but indelible, brush with prejudice.

"At an early age, I found out I was different. I was Portuguese," he recalls. "My parents were immigrants. We lived in the Hollow section of Bridgeport, a neighborhood that was predominantly Irish and Italian. The Irish woman across the street was always calling me, 'You Portuguese bastard.'"

Many neighborhood youngsters showered similar abuse on the little kid with the swarthy complexion. After Florindo had blackened a few eyes and scuffled with the Italian and Irish kids, they began to call him Porty and then Porky. Porky stuck.

"I fought every damn day. My brother, Gus, God rest his soul, told me, 'You've got to stop fighting everyone.'"

Agousto "Goose" Vieira, a gentle, soft-spoken man who was to pitch in the Cubs farm system, directed his pugnacious younger brother to the Boys Club. It was there that Porky decided to channel his energy into basketball.

"When I saw my name in print for the first time—it was just a little thing—I knew that was it. I just had to be the best," he says.

The progression was rapid. From Middle Street, for which he played in abbreviated eighty-five-pounder games between halves of NBA games at the old Madison Square Garden and Boston Garden, he advanced to Central High School. The Hilltoppers were coached by one of the Park City's legends, Eddie Reilly.

"He didn't know a lot about basketball, but he knew how to motivate kids," Porky says. "He was a tough old Irish guy, too. He was still catching BP [batting practice] at sixty-seven and handling tackling dummies."

The referee handing the ball to Sacred Heart's Darrin Robinson is none other than Frank "Porky" Vieira. The diminutive Vieira still holds Quinnipiac records with 68 points in a game and 32.8 PPG for his career. The six-two Robinson is the Sacred Heart record holder in both departments, with 55 points in a game and 27 PPG for his career (1989–93). *Courtesy of Sacred Heart University Sports Information.*

The Hilltoppers had older, brighter stars during that New England championship season—Ronnie DelBianco, Alvin Clinkscales and diminutive Ernie Petrucciano, who, at five-four, whipped behind-the-back passes to teammates. Porky was the team's sixth man.

Vieira says, "DelBianco was a tough, tough SOB. He was All-State in basketball and football, and he signed a bonus contract with the Pirates as a catcher. Clinkscales was the [Bill] Russell of the fifties. He was a zone by himself. And Ernie was a point guard before there were point guards. He was a legend.

"We used to scrimmage the Fairfield U's and the UB's; they were pretty good, and we used to beat the crap out of them."

A lot of people believe those Hilltoppers could have done well in any era. Their accomplishments were significant—back-to-back runner-up finishes in the state Class A tournament (Clinkscales missed the 1950 title game with bronchitis), the New England championship in Boston. However, when Vieira reached his zenith as a senior by averaging 28 points per game, Central was declared ineligible for the state tournament. One of the team's stars was discovered to be overage.

"I'm so thankful to have been brought up in Bridgeport at that time," he says. "I never played in a high school game that didn't have standing-room-only crowds. At the old Central, which is now the city hall, we had to shoot between the girders. We played a lot of our games at the Bridgeport Armory, now the [Cardinal] Shehan Center. When we came back from Boston after winning the championship, there were hundreds of people waiting on Golden Hill Street."

The low point in Vieira's life came between high school and his arrival at Quinnipiac. He "bombed out" at Arnold College, drifted from factory to factory and played industrial league basketball for Sikorsky. "I even lost my first high school sweetheart." A lot of time was wasted in diners and pool halls.

Enter Florindo Vieira Sr. "My dad worked forty-one years at Bridgeport Brass. He took me to the rolling mills for two weeks. I didn't know what he was doing at the time, but he was telling me, in his way, that I'd better get a college education. That was a major awakening for me. When you're out there, nobody cares. You're only as good as your last game. I saw guys go the other way, and that's putting it mildly."

The late Tuffie Maroon, who doubled as basketball coach and sports publicist, brought Vieira to Quinnipiac in 1953. A wonderful decision for all parties. Reunited with Petrucciano, Porky proceeded to electrify New England with his scoring outbursts. As a freshman, he averaged 37.1 points per game, second in the nation behind Clarence "Bevo" Francis of Rio Grande.

When Petrucciano departed for the service, Porky slipped a bit the next two seasons, if scoring averages of 31.5 and 29.1 can be construed as subpar. But he accumulated points at a more prolific 34.9 pace as a senior in 1957, losing the national scoring title by three-tenths of a point.

Remembers Petrucciano: "He was one of the greatest shooters to come out of the state. He had all the shots...jump shot, set shot, driving hook shot from the right side. Would he be great today? Certainly. There are more little guys playing today than in our time. If you were great then, you'd be great today."

Although Quinnipiac played less than a heavyweight schedule, Vieira was selected to play in the 1957 East-West College All-Star Game at Madison Square Garden. This was the opportunity for Porky to display his prowess against the nation's major college stars, before the eyes of NBA scouts, but alas, it wasn't to be. A pre-game injury in practice prevented Vieira from playing.

"I was going through a screen and [Louisville's] Charlie Tyra, who was built like a house, stuck out his knee. They called it strained tendons," Porky remembers. "That blew the game for me and a guaranteed tour with the Harlem Globetrotters."

Although the mighty mite was unable to display his exceptional wares in the NBA, he spent the next five seasons in the semipro Connecticut State Basketball League. Often he was paid $150 a game. Always he delivered.

The competition included "the dumpers": seven-foot Bill Spivey of Kentucky and Jack Molinas of Columbia; the predominantly black Milford Chiefs with Bobby Knight, Frank Keitt and Clinkscales; the Columbus Auto Body Bears of New Haven with Richie Kross, the Davins brothers and Dick Surhoff. Even an NBA team or two in an exhibition game.

Nobody stopped Vieira. That was especially true the night he erupted for 89 points—a personal high at any level (and *before* the 3-point goal)— when the Savoys defeated the Red Embers of Manchester, 129–125, in overtime in a CSBL game. The date was March 8, 1959.

When Don Ormrod asked Vieira to join him at little New Haven College as head baseball coach and assistant basketball coach, Porky decided it was time to pack away his uniform for keeps, even though he was just twenty-eight years old. "Hey," he reasoned, "I was teaching at St. Anthony's [High School] in Bristol. When you get a chance to coach in college, you take it."

Ormrod's offer came with several caveats: "No more [playing] basketball. Stop swearing every second sentence. Wear a tie. And enough of this silly nickname. You're Frank Vieira now."

Vieira followed the rules, at least most of the time. "Don Ormrod gave me the opportunity to become a college coach and he gave my brother Gus a job [as pitching coach]. The school doesn't owe me. I owe the school."

Would Florindo Francesco "Porky" Vieira do anything differently? His answer comes without hesitation. "I was a good-looking baseball prospect. When I was in high school, Chick Genovese of the New York Giants wanted to give me $1,000 to sign. The New York Giants! But I told him no. Later, Whitey Piurek of the Brooklyn Dodgers tried to sign me. The only regret I have was to have gotten my chance in pro ball."

Vieira makes occasional visits to the city of his birth to spend time with his mother, Conception, who is in her eightieth year. She lives on Arlington Street in the North End. His father, Gus and a sister are gone now.

For a moment, Porky's eyes become misty. "I was lucky," he says. "My two greatest heroes were my father and my brother, Gus, and they were always there for me."

Bridgeport Light, October 18, 1989

WILLIAMSON'S LEARNING PROCESS CONTINUES

NAUGATUCK—Wendell Ladner did not die in vain. John Williamson is living proof.

The tragic crash of Eastern Airlines' Flight 66 near New York's Kennedy International Airport on June 24 snuffed out the lives of 114 people, including the New York Nets' forward, but Williamson doesn't plan to forget his teammate and friend.

Ladner, white and Mississippi born, and Williamson, black and the product of a New Haven ghetto, couldn't have come from more diverse backgrounds. And yet there was a bond.

"I was our physical guard, he was our physical forward. I knew him very well, used to party with him. Still today I can't believe he's gone," Williamson recalled this week during a visit to the Borough playgrounds. "I'm from the city, he was from Mississippi where they had all that racial stuff," he continued. "When two players meet like that, you accomplish a lot."

Williamson, the offense-minded guard with the powerful six-two, two-hundred-pound physique and wide assortment of shots, has grown considerably since his days at New Haven's Wilbur Cross High School in

John Williamson was virtually unstoppable wherever he played. *Courtesy of Nets Basketball.*

the late 1960s. But his growth cannot be measured by a ruler.

As a youngster growing up in the lower Grand Avenue area, Williamson dealt in stereotypes: "All white people are bad." After attending the predominantly white New Mexico State University and playing professionally in the American Basketball Association, both with and against whites, for the past two years, he realizes that stereotypes, while convenient, are inaccurate. "You have just as many good whites as you have bad whites," Williamson says today. "You have just as many good blacks as bad blacks."

Williamson's visit to the area is a combination of business and pleasure. "Super John," as he's been known since he was scoring 30, 40 and 50 points in a game at Wilbur Cross, is preparing to operate a basketball camp at the Naugatuck Middle School next week.

His partner in the venture is Bill Rado Jr., who is to Naugatuck High basketball what John Williamson is to Cross basketball. Some fifty boys have been enrolled thus far; they hope to add others before the camp opens on Monday morning.

When Williamson and Rado met recently, it was inevitable that they would get together on the basketball court. John came away from their one-on-one confrontation a narrow—and surprised—victor. "He's really tough for his age," Williamson said of the thirty-two-year-old Rado, who had starred at the University of Georgia. "The main thing is he's got a deadly jump shot. I underestimated it at first. He's got the talent. He should have been a professional."

John Williamson, 1975 Topps card. *Courtesy of Frank Corr.*

Williamson keeps his own talents sharp by playing in two summer leagues in New York City, the widely known Rucker Pro in Harlem and the Bill Douglas League in Queens. His teammates and opponents read like a who's who of professional basketball: Nate Archibald, Marvin Barnes, Larry Kenon, Brian Winters, Bill Schaeffer, Tom Riker, Harthorne Wingo, Mel Davis, John Shumate, Ed Searcy, et al.

A rookie sensation with the 1973–74 Nets, who captured the ABA title, John hopes to augment his scoring skills with increased production in other areas. "I want to be a good all-around player. I'm trying to shoot better than 75 percent from all areas; be a good assists man, setup man, a good rebounding man. My main objective is to be a good, top defensive man. You can't just be a shooter. When you find a guy who can do everything, like Billy Cunningham, Jerry West, Dr. J., he's so much more valuable."

Williamson, like so many others, stands in awe of the man they call Dr. J., Julius Erving. The six-six forward with the uncanny leaping ability has dominated the ABA the past four seasons; many regard him as the finest player in the game today.

"Doctor is the best," Williamson said, firmly. "His movements on the court send a sensation through my body. Inspires you. But he has personality off the court. He sits down and talks to people."

John's scoring average fell off from 14.5 to 11.5 last winter, mainly because of knee surgery that restricted his playing time much of the year. Still, he shot 60 percent from the floor during the ABA Eastern Division playoffs, although the Nets were ousted by the Spirits of St. Louis in five games.

The Players

How good will the 1975–76 Nets be?

"We should be so much better this year," he said. "We have the number one rebounder in the league in [Swen] Nater. To get the fast breaks, get the patterns working, you need a strong center."

With the six-eleven Nater, obtained from San Antonio in the trade for Kenon, added to the likes of Erving, Williamson, Billy Paultz, Brian Taylor and Al Skinner, and a first-rate rookie in Maryland's Maurice Lucas, the Nets shape up as a contender.

Coach Kevin Loughery, in Williamson's eyes, is a big asset, too. "He doesn't inspire me 100 percent," said Super John. "He inspires me 115 percent."

Waterbury Republican, July 12, 1975

CHAPTER 3
The Coaches

THE PASSING OF A STAGS LEGEND

The guy could flat-out coach. Even his detractors would admit that. Until the arrival of the Big East, he was able to attract some high-profile players to Fairfield University, notably All–New York City guard Joe DeSantis, six-ten Mark Young and three Connecticut All-Staters, Steve Balkun, Owen Mahorn and Mark Plefka.

Together, they helped transform the low-budget Stags into an eastern heavyweight that competed in three National Invitation Tournaments in a six-year span and played before capacity crowds in Alumni Hall— before the tiny campus gym even had a name.

Yes, Fred Barakat made an indelible mark during his eleven seasons (1970–81) as Fairfield's head coach. On Monday, he suffered a fatal heart attack at a hospital in Greensboro, North Carolina. He was seventy-one.

For several years, Fred and I were as close as a coach and media type can be. As sports editor, and then executive sports editor, of the *Waterbury Republican-American*, I chronicled his entire career at the Jesuit college. I witnessed many of the highs and the lows during this period.

At times, he could be charming and funny. His wife, Florence, was a sweetheart, and it was Flo who introduced me to the woman who would become my wife and the mother of our three children. That auspicious meeting is embedded in my consciousness. March 18, 1973. That afternoon, Fairfield had upset Marshall, 80–76, in the tournament's

Coach Fred Barakat at work, with 1980 captain Jerome "Flip" Williams at right. *Courtesy of Fairfield University Sports Information.*

opening round, and the Stags coaches, athletic administrators and guests went to celebrate at the NIT dinner at Mama Leone's. For Patti and me, it was love at first sight, or at least second glance. Some six months later, Fred was among the speakers at my bachelor dinner in Waterbury. Patti and I were married that October.

The highlights of Barakat's coaching career would fill volumes. The three NITs (1973, 1974, 1978). The landmark 123–103 rout of fourteenth-in-the-nation Holy Cross in January 1978 en route to a 22-5 record. Back-to-back victories over UConn—which prompted the Huskies to drop Fairfield from their schedule for two seasons. A double-overtime win over Detroit in Madison Square Garden. Noteworthy road victories over Georgetown, Boston College, Holy Cross, Villanova, St. Bonaventure and other eastern teams of stature. A school-record 160 wins (against 128 losses) on a nickel-and-dime budget.

John Ryan, who was the creative point guard on the Stags' first two NIT teams, had a chance meeting with his former coach in Hartford this past winter. Barakat was there as an invited guest for the fortieth anniversary of Dee Rowe's first UConn squad, which won the Yankee

Fairfield point guard John Ryan handles the ball against Virginia Tech in the quarterfinals of the 1973 NIT at Madison Square Garden. Tech pulled out a 77–76 squeaker and went on to win the title. If the NCAA had tabulated assists during Ryan's era, he might have led the nation as a senior when he averaged 11.6 per game in 1973–74. *Courtesy of Fairfield University Sports Information.*

Conference title. Fred had spent the 1969–70 season as a Rowe assistant prior to accepting the Fairfield job.

"He looked terrific. He was the picture of health," Ryan recalled. "He invited me to play golf with him in North Carolina. We talked about having a reunion for our 1973 [NIT] team."

Ryan, who lives in Fairfield with his family and is a media buyer with Gaskell Media Management in Guilford, called Barakat "a player's coach." "If you were a point guard, he'd listen to you," Ryan said. "I'd always come off the court and talk to him. Who doesn't like to be empowered?"

Don Cook, now the executive director of athletics at neighboring Sacred Heart University, was hired as Fairfield's athletic director in 1971, shortly after Fred had completed his first year as coach. Their relationship was strained at times, but Cook always respected Barakat the coach.

"I thought he was well prepared, had a great knowledge of the game's Xs and Os, and never did I see him get out-coached by anyone, even some of the greats we faced like Dave Gavitt," Cook said. (Georgetown's John Thompson, BC's Tom Davis and Villanova's Rollie Massimino

Florence Barakat is flanked by her son, Ricky, and George Bisacca during Fairfield University's tribute to her late husband, Fred Barakat, at the Webster Bank Arena in Bridgeport on February 19, 2011. Bisacca, in his final year as athletic director, hired Barakat as head coach. Ray Kelly (with mustache) was among some two dozen former Stags players in attendance. "It was an emotional time, a beautiful time," Florence said of the ceremony. *Courtesy of Fairfield University Sports Information.*

belong in that august group, too.) "He brought the Fairfield program to a national level with the NITs and the Holiday Festival. We got tremendous publicity because of it."

After he left Fairfield, there was a trace of irony in Barakat's next position. The coach who had once harassed referees was appointed coordinator of officials for the Atlantic Coast Conference. He would spend a quarter century in the ACC's employ and retired in 2007 as associate commissioner.

Fred, thanks for the memories. May you rest in peace.

Daily Fairfield, June 23, 2010

A WARM LOOK AT A GOLD KEY WINNER

EAST HAVEN—The building has been enlarged and renovated more than once to accommodate additional students. Most of the teachers are new. Tyler Street seems narrower, a far less imposing boulevard. But Frank Crisafi, the man we called "Coach," doesn't change.

He is fifty-four years old and in his thirty-first year as head basketball coach and director of athletics at East Haven High School. He remains coach, friend, counselor and, in some cases, father figure to hundreds of youngsters.

Frank Crisafi, East Haven High School's legendary coach and athletic director. *Courtesy of Frank Crisafi.*

For this old alumnus, class of '57, and wayward basketball player (he never did truly appreciate my hook shot), it is always a pleasure to see the man. Today, the pleasure is doubled. Crisafi has been selected to receive a Gold Key Award from the Connecticut Sports Writers' Alliance, and I want to hear his reaction as well as his reminisces of 1,001 games.

I am not disappointed. His reaction is as I expect it to be. Warm words of gratitude and thanks. "I'm very thankful." "Probably one of the greatest awards I've ever received, and I've been lucky to receive many of them." And a bit later: "It means more than any of them…"

To say this award is long overdue is trite. One has heard this phrase countless times whenever somebody is handing somebody else a trophy. But in the case of Frank Leonard Crisafi, it's true. The writers—of which I am a card-carrying member and even a past president—have been remiss. He should have been honored long ago.

Let's look at the Crisafi record:

Football, the sport he reluctantly relinquished following the 1976 season: 181 wins, 84 losses, 11 ties. One undefeated season (1952) and nine years with just one loss. Mario Mozzillo, Dom Pettinicchi, Hank Luzzi, Joel Gustafson, John DeCaprio, Bob Vetrone, Terry Holcombe, Jerry Iannotti, Marty DiMezza, Mike DeMarco, Bill Kotowski, Joe Scalabrino and Mike Zito, All-Staters all.

Crisafi said: "The team I remember the most—although it didn't have the best record—was the one in 1951. That was [quarterback] Ronnie

Rossetti's year. We were undefeated, untied and unscored upon going into Thanksgiving morning. Branford beat us. We were leading 6–0 and then got beat on the old sleeper play. They made the extra point and we lost, 7–6."

Basketball: 485 wins, 179 losses, five Class B (now Class M) state titles and one Class B New England championship. Tony Massari, Red O'Mara, Teddy Sullivan, Dick Ezold, Ralph Paolillo, John DeCaprio, Bob Vetrone, Sal Paolillo, Bruce Larsen, Phil Andros, Mike DeMarco, Bob Warner and Al Carfora, All-Staters all. Most remarkably, the seventy-seven-game winning streak that began with the opening game of the 1953–54 season and ended, melodramatically, in the state championship game of 1956—a 62–60 loss to Stonington and its unstoppable six-seven center, Wayne Lawrence.

With so many championship teams (1954, '55, '57, '60, '63) and other talented squads (the Easties were state runners-up in 1953, '56 and '58), Crisafi hesitates to name the one best. Finally, he does. "The best was the one that won the Housatonic League, state and New England championships in 1954. I think we were the only Class B team in Connecticut that ever won the New England title."

That was the team of Massari, twice an All-State forward and still the holder of many East Haven scoring records, and O'Mara. Crisafi believes Massari was "very much ahead of his time" as a percentage shooter. He was sinking better than half his shots at a time when most of the premier NBA players were in the 33 to 38 percent range. "Anthony would go home on game days and shoot after school. I had to chase him off the court he had in his backyard." Massari parlayed his fluid jump shot and brainpower into a Harvard education.

While titles have eluded Crisafi-coached basketball teams in recent years, he still puts forth scrappy, well-drilled squads. The 1975–76 Yellow Jackets, featuring a one-man scoring machine named Al Carfora, went 20-2 and made some noise in the Class L state tournament.

In his early years, Frank coached the East Haven baseball team with some success, and golf came under his jurisdiction in recent spring seasons. But basketball and football remain his primary interests.

Is coaching any more difficult today than when he began in 1947? Crisafi prefers to say the challenges are different. "The kids today are a little more inquisitive. You have to have the answers for them. Maybe they're a little smarter," he said. "In the old days, if I told them black was white and white was black, they'd believe me.

"Every kid wants to win, that hasn't changed," he continued. "The kids are just as competitive, but they don't want to work as hard."

Although born in New Haven, Crisafi has always considered East Haven home. Except for military service during World War II and his undergraduate days at Arnold College in Milford, he's seldom left. He considers himself such a "sentimentalist" that "I'd never give a second thought to leaving."

Indeed, he and wife Gloria still live in the small, neat home at the corner of Thompson Avenue and Frank Street. There are three Crisafi children, athletes all: Eddie, twenty-five; Fran, twenty-two; and Susie, fifteen.

Oh, there were opportunities to move on, at least two of which, he says, were "in the palm of my hand." In the 1950s, Brown University wanted to hire him as head basketball coach. "Before that, I could have gone with Hugh Greer as his assistant at Connecticut. We were very close."

But Frank Crisafi decided to stay put. And now his staying power has been rewarded with the Gold Key.

I dare say that on the night of January 16, 1978, hundreds of his admirers and former players will be there for him at the Hartford Civic Center when the writers present him their coveted key. Congratulations, Coach.

Waterbury American, December 1, 1977

UPDATE: Frank Crisafi went out on a high note, coaching East Haven to its sixth state title in his final season with a 63–57 overtime victory over Bullard-Havens of Bridgeport in the Class L championship game on March 14, 1980. He retired with a 525-196 (.729) record.

DETRICK SAYS GOLD KEY PART OF HIS LUCKY YEAR

"This is my lucky year," Bill Detrick said.

Well, yes.

This past weekend, this veteran coach of more than five hundred basketball games was inducted into the Central Connecticut State College Hall of Fame. And now there will be the Gold Key, the award given by the Connecticut Sports Writers' Alliance. Detrick will be among three key recipients at the writers' annual dinner on Sunday, January 27, in New Haven.

"I'm pretty happy, very happy about this. I don't think you win an award like this if you bounce around a lot," he said.

Well, Bill Detrick isn't one to bounce around. This is his twenty-first season as Central Connecticut's head coach, a reign of both length and achievement. The Detrick won-lost record, including two games this season, is a bright 331-173, and some of New England's finest college division teams have been assembled by this man.

There was a four-year stretch, 1962 to 1966, when the Blue Devils won eighty-eight games and lost but ten. Yes, ten. That marvelous 1965–66 team, the team of Gene Reilly, Jim Muraski, Paul Zajac, Stan Pelcher and Bob Plosky, went 23-3, captured the District I NCAA College Division title and represented the region in the national tournament at Evansville, Indiana. Unfortunately, the eventual champion, Kentucky Wesleyan, was Central's first obstacle. The score, 84–76, was close.

"We'd had some great teams. That was probably our best team," Detrick said. "The coach of that Kentucky Wesleyan team, Guy Strong, told me that this Kentucky Wesleyan team was better than most of his Division I teams."

Detrick, the coach, is regarded as a master technician and innovator. He is a motivator; 331 wins, four NCAA bids, a New England College Division Coach of the Year Award (in 1966) and countless lesser salutes attest to his coaching prowess.

But he is equally proud that so many of his former players have joined him in the coaching ranks. In every section of the state there is a Detrick disciple coaching—and coaching well—on the high school level. Start with Tom LaBella, holder of Connecticut's record for consecutive victories, at Middletown High. And then proceed to Joe Haberl at Torrington, Mike Pennella at New London, Bill Reagan at Old Saybrook, Joe Cirello at Stonington, George Linn at New Britain, Reilly at Portland.

All learned from Bill Detrick. And so have a number of college coaches. Howie Dickenman, a Division II All-American in 1969, is the number one assistant at Canisius. Pelcher is an assistant at Springfield College. Jim Kelly, a 1971–72 co-captain, is assisting Bob Zuffelato (an earlier Central athlete) at Marshall, and Dan Switchenko is the head coach at Alma College. John Salerno, the Mattatuck Community College athletic director and former coach, was the co-captain of Detrick's 1964–65 squad.

Central Connecticut State's Bill Detrick celebrates his 300ᵗʰ coaching victory with co-captains Jim Cassell, *center*, and Jeri Quinn on February 2, 1977. *Courtesy of Central Connecticut State Sports Information.*

There was a time when Detrick had coaching aspirations elsewhere, but that doesn't seem to be the case anymore. He was a candidate for various jobs at the major college level; he came close at several places. "The only good, bona fide offer I had," he admits, "was from Roanoke. The guy sent me a plane ticket, and I chickened out.

"When the time came to move, I wasn't ready to move. When I wanted to move, there wasn't any move. Truthfully, I haven't had any better [coaching situations] than Central."

Detrick, now fifty-two, is a native of Springfield, New Jersey. He left the Garden State to attend Central (then New Britain State Teachers College) in the late 1940s. In effect, he's been on campus ever since, although he did coach at the high school level for a few seasons.

He was an all-around athlete at Central, a quarterback and end on the football team, a first baseman on the baseball squad and a six-foot forward "who pushed like hell" on the basketball court. His baseball skills were such that he played professionally, as a third baseman, with Torrington of the Class B Colonial League. "When the league folded," he chuckled, "I folded."

Litchfield High served as his first proving ground as a basketball coach. It was a small school, but the basketball, he recalled, "really was a pretty big thing." His three-year record there was 46-18, and his 1953–54 squad won the league championship and lost to Morgan of Clinton in the semifinals of the Class C state tournament.

"The thing I remember most about Litchfield was the facility, the Center School," he said. "The stage was still on the floor, and the basket was there. When you filled the place, it was a fantastic thing."

Detrick's wife, the former Barbara Ferguson, and their three children, Sara, Barbara and Debbie, plan to be there at the Sheraton Park Plaza in New Haven to share the proud moment when the Blue Devils coach is presented the coveted key. If you would like to join them on the final Sunday in January, tickets (priced at twenty dollars) are available from the *American* sports department.

"My father, who is eighty years old, came up when I received the Hall of Fame award at the college," Detrick said. "I told him, 'I'm going to get another award, Pop.' When you're joining people like the immortals who have the Gold Key, it's pretty special."

Many will insist that Bill Detrick is pretty special, too.

Waterbury American, December 5, 1979

IN DEFENSE OF ROWE

It has become fashionable of late to throw verbal darts in the direction of Dee Rowe. Apparently because he doesn't have a 172-0 coaching record and the University of Connecticut isn't challenging Indiana for national supremacy.

A certain element among the fans has taken to chanting "Hump Dee, Dump Dee" whenever the Huskies appear on the verge of losing, which isn't especially often but apparently too often to suit the dissidents. Such sophisticated thinking.

At least one UConn partisan, a recent graduate of the state university, has vented his displeasure in a somewhat lengthy letter to a Connecticut newspaper. He writes of "serious deficiencies" in his alma mater's basketball program, calling it a "deplorable situation." And now a columnist who knows neither the man nor the situation has gotten on his soapbox.

Gad, you would think UConn was being coached by a combination Bill Musselman–Beryl Shipley–Jerry Tarkanian. That, worse, UConn hasn't won a basketball game since Sumner Dole.

Let's examine some of those accusations and see how they hold up under scrutiny:

Charge: Under Rowe, the UConn basketball program has deteriorated into mediocrity. Fact: Under Rowe, the Huskies have regained much of their lost New England prestige and have rivaled, and occasionally surpassed, the achievements of the Fred Shabel era. In nearly seven seasons as head coach, Dee Rowe has assembled a 97-75 won-lost record, solid in itself. But in the last four years, or since he has been working exclusively with his recruits, the Rowe record is a more imposing 65-35. In that period, only one other major college coach in the

Three of the Nutmeg State's basketball notables were the Gold Key recipients at the Connecticut Sports Writers Alliance's thirty-seventh annual dinner in Hartford on January 16, 1978. *From left*: Dee Rowe, shot maker (and baseball coach) extraordinaire Porky Vieira and East Haven High Coach Frank Crisafi. *Tom Kabelka / courtesy of* Waterbury Republican-American.

region, Providence's Dave Gavitt, has a higher winning percentage.

Nineteen victories in 1973–74, eighteen last season and probably something in that neighborhood this year hardly smacks of deterioration.

Charge: Connecticut, under Rowe, plays an inferior schedule. Fact: While UConn does not play a so-called "national schedule," neither does any other New England team with the notable exception of Providence. Under Rowe, UConn does compete against more first-rate opposition than did the Shabel teams, simply because nearly every Yankee Conference team has improved significantly in the past decade. Vermont, for example, used to have trouble beating Norwich but now competes against the likes of Ohio State and Duke and occasionally

UConn Coach Dee Rowe confers with his prize pupil, Tony Hanson. *Courtesy of University of Connecticut Athletic Communications.*

defeats Connecticut. Massachusetts has reached its peak in the last several years, and New Hampshire and Maine are more competitive.

Charge: Rowe has won only one of five post-season games. Fact: True, but at least he's getting them there. In its entire intercollegiate history, Connecticut has participated in three National Invitation Tournaments, and Rowe was at the helm in two of them.

Charge: Rowe doesn't win the games he's supposed to win. True, in a few cases, but he also wins some games he has no business winning. Two years ago, UConn ended Syracuse's thirty-seven-game home court winning streak and stunned St. John's in the NIT. Virtually the same Rutgers team that is breezing through the current season without a loss tasted defeat in Storrs last year, and UMass was upended on its home court in each of the last two seasons. That victory over a 15-4 Lafayette team in Madison Square Garden a couple of nights ago wasn't a bad piece of work either.

Charge: Too many of the state's outstanding high school players, including Tom Roy and Bruce Campbell, slipped

away from UConn and wound up elsewhere. Fact: Too many of the state's outstanding high school players couldn't—or didn't—get past the admissions office in Storrs. And while Roy and Campbell got away, Tony Hanson, Al Weston, Joe Whelton and Jim Abromaitis cast their lot with Connecticut. Ask Fairfield's Fred Barakat how badly he wanted Hanson and, to a slightly lesser extent, Whelton and Abro.

Summation: Dee Rowe might not be the strategist John Wooden was or possess the selling techniques of a Lefty Driesell or a Gavitt, either of whom could reap a profit with an ice cube stand in the Antarctic. He's made a few coaching blunders (what coach hasn't?), and his recent teams, while exciting, sometimes lack cohesion on the court. But Donald E. "Dee" Rowe scores high in many areas. He is an honest, fair, straightforward man in a profession in which chameleons abound. He is well respected by his peers; such diverse types as Gavitt, Barakat, Bob Cousy and Assumption's Andy Laska are among his close friends.

As coach and man, Dee Rowe outranks a lot of people, and I, for one, am proud to have an association with him.

Waterbury Republican, February 15, 1976

TAYLOR KEEPS WINNING IN PERSPECTIVE

Harrison Taylor's world has changed little since that Saturday afternoon in March when Bassick High School completed its marvelous undefeated championship season, when his Lions disposed of Warren Harding, 76–72, in double overtime to capture the Class L state title.

He still comes to work each morning at the Ben Franklin Education Center on Kossuth Street, located just a pelota toss from the jai alai fronton. You will find him sitting behind the desk in Room 315, teaching social studies and science to a small group of students.

"These are ninth- and tenth-grade kids," he explains. "Small classes. We try to improve their attention span, so they can be mainstreamed into the high schools later on. They've got to be able to read so they can become productive. Everything's going to automation. If you aren't productive in life, crime breeds crime."

The building is in need of a face-lift, and there is litter outside the front door. The only fresh paint on the exterior walls of the Ben Franklin

Education Center is the graffiti. You have to care about kids to teach here, in this "alternative" high school, and it is clear that Harrison Taylor cares.

When he deems the situation appropriate, he will "go to a kid's home to give my side of the story, especially if I know the parents."

The coach of the state's reigning Class L state championship team—now certifiably one of the great high school basketball teams in Bridgeport's proud history—presents a gruff exterior to those he mistrusts, but there is a soft side, a caring side.

"Some people," points out Bernie Lofton, his number one assistant at Bassick, "wouldn't see that. They see him as strict and stern. This year's team brought out the soft side in him, even before they started winning."

Harrison Taylor is not your stereotypical basketball coach, or at least the coach we see in our mind's eye. The glasses, the bald head and the trim mustache help form the picture of the social studies and science teacher, which he is.

But athletics, and especially basketball, always were important to this man approaching forty, who began life in Pittsburgh as the son of Moses and the late Vera Taylor. He was "four or five" when the family moved to Bridgeport and took up residence in the P.T. Barnum housing project.

At Bassick, he played defensive end in football and point guard in basketball. "I was known for my defensive skills in basketball," he says, smiling. "Some say I was physical; I just played hard."

Harvey Herer, just a few years removed from the University of Bridgeport, was beginning his basketball coaching tenure with the Lions when Taylor arrived. "Harrison played on a very

Surrounded by his jubilant players, Bassick Coach Harrison Taylor holds aloft the 1988–89 state championship plaque. *Ed Brinsko* / Bridgeport Light.

good team in an era when there were a lot of great players," Herer recalls. "Central had Gene Mack and Tom Sparks. Fairfield Prep had the kid [Jim] Fitzsimmons, who played in the Dapper Dan. We had Jeff—or Chucky—Howard. In another year, Harrison would have been considered a great player. Instead he was considered good."

Good enough to make the 1968 MBIAC all-star team when the league embraced Prep and the Milford schools, hard-nosed enough to play at Champlain Junior College in Burlington, Vermont, and later at North Carolina A&T.

Taylor gestures to his team. *Ed Brinsko / Bridgeport Light.*

Being one of the few blacks in Burlington, he says, "was an experience. Taking a kid out of the P.T. Barnum apartments…"

He left Champlain after a year and drifted, but not for long. "My mother made me get out. My father told me to go into the service or go back to school. I did the smart thing. I chose to go back to school."

There is a strong work ethic in the Taylor family and a belief in education. Moses Taylor, who held down two jobs, was a black All-American football player at Bluefield State in West Virginia during the early 1940s. Vera Taylor also went to college, as did a grandmother and a great-grandfather. And so Harrison landed at North Carolina A&T and eventually earned a teaching certificate from Sacred Heart University and a master's from UB.

Basketball remained an integral part of his life, too. He began coaching in the playgrounds "when I was fourteen" and organized a summer league at Beardsley Terrace, attracting teams from New Haven (with Super John Williamson), Providence (with Marvin Barnes) and elsewhere. "I coached Frank Oleynick and Barry McLeod at the West End Youth Center when they were twelve," he recalls. "People don't remember, but Barry was a better ballplayer then."

Harrison Taylor often served as the unofficial PA announcer for those Urban Coalition summer games. In *Chase the Game*, Pat Jordan's superb tribute to Messrs. Oleynick, McLeod and Walter Luckett, Oleynick describes Harrison "as a fighter. He had a lot of respect in the city. He'd do a play-by-play thing during the game. He'd call Walter 'Doctor,' and he called me and Barry 'Butch Cassidy and the Sundance Kid.'"

Taylor credits Bud Knittel, whom he assisted at Bassick during the 1970s, with imparting valuable lessons in Coaching 101. "He taught me the game. He taught me how to use the clock to my advantage." Later, he coached under the remarkable Charlie Bentley—his friend—at Harding before becoming his own man at Bassick seven years ago.

Bassick All-Stater Harper Williams cuts down the net. Four years later, as a University of Massachusetts senior, he was voted Most Valuable Player of the Atlantic Ten Tournament won by the Minutemen. He scored 1,534 points in his four-year career at UMass. *Ed Brinsko* / Bridgeport Light.

He would lose seventeen straight games to Bentley's Presidents before the 1988–89 Bassick team of Harper Williams, Jerome Johnson, Louie Kinchen, Angel Echevarria, Cory Smith, Eric Geer and the rest played the avenger. They defeated Harding three times this season, twice before capacity crowds at UB and then the big one in March at Central Connecticut State University in New Britain.

"I've seen some great Harding teams, some great Central teams. But of all the teams I've seen since 1964, I would place this Bassick team among the top five," Taylor says.

"It [winning the Lions' first state title since 1940] wasn't something we didn't know we were going to do. We had planned to win the state championship. We didn't think we'd go undefeated. I look at that as more of a great achievement."

Does Harrison Taylor feel blessed to have been given this once-in-a-lifetime coaching opportunity?

"Blessed?!" He thinks for a moment. "Yes," he finally answers, "I've been blessed. I'll forever call this my dream team."

Bridgeport Light, April 19, 1989

END OF AN ERA AT YALE

It has been said that a man must be a good pitcher to lose twenty games, or otherwise he wouldn't be given the opportunity to work often enough to lose that number. When one examines the list of twenty-game losers, he discovers Bobo Newsom, Hugh Mulcahy, Murry Dickson, Roger Craig, Al Jackson, Wilbur Wood—all rather good, a few even outstanding, pitchers. Even the incomparable Walter Johnson once dropped twenty-five games in a season.

Under the same premise, it can be argued that Joe Vancisin was such a good basketball coach that he lost more games than any Yale coach in history. If he hadn't been held in high esteem, he wouldn't have been on the job for nineteen seasons, and he wouldn't have been around long enough to lose 242 games.

He also wouldn't have been at courtside long enough to win 206 games and produce two Ivy League championships.

When Vancisin's resignation takes effect on the first day of July, an era will end at Yale. The scholarly, gentlemanly basketball coach who

Joe Vancisin was a familiar sight on the Yale sidelines for nineteen seasons. *Courtesy of Yale University Sports Information.*

popularized the "Shuffle" offense, the man who spent three months in the Sudan as part of a cultural exchange program and conducted clinics in such exotic locales as Taiwan, Malaysia, Japan, Hawaii and Okinawa, will be gone from the Payne Whitney Gym.

His critics—whose number includes fans, alumni, members of the media, even some of his own players—insist his departure is long overdue. There are others, a decided minority, who wish he had stayed on another year or two, at least until he had another winner.

Eighteen months ago, when I was in the process of preparing an article about Vancisin for the Yale football program—yes, football—he mentioned an ambition to climb higher. "Like any coach," he said, "you're looking for advancement, getting into some administrative position. I want an upward move. Basketball coaching would be a lateral movement. I'm still young enough to be an administrator some place. I have some unique experiences to offer somebody."

Yale's 1956–57 team won the Ivy League title behind a first-year coach, Joe Vancisin. *Front row, from left*: Alki Scopelitis, Tom Molumphy, Captain Ed Robinson, Tom Sargent, George Thompson. *Second row*: Vancisin, Al Sheals, Bill Bodman, Jim Whelplay, Johnny Lee, manager Richard Hall. *Third row*: Trainer Eugene "Whitey" Fitzsimmons, Nolan Baird, Ted Kurtz, Larry Downs, Don Bab, Sterling Harwell, assistant manager Emory Buck. *Courtesy of Yale University Sports Information.*

The administrative position will become reality when he assumes his new position as executive secretary of the National Association of Basketball Coaches, an organization he once served as president.

There was a time when losing basketball teams weren't synonymous with Joe Vancisin. As a high school player, he was the captain and floor leader of the 1939–40 Bassick of Bridgeport team that captured the state Class A and New England Tournament titles. Four years later, he was a senior on a 19-2 Dartmouth squad that advanced to the NCAA Tournament championship game against Utah (he scored four points in the Big Green's 42–40 overtime loss).

As a head coach, Vancisin was regarded as something of a genius at the outset, winning two league championships and finishing in a first-place tie

Left: Johnny Lee's all-around play was a driving force behind Yale's 1956–57 Ivy League champions. *Courtesy of Yale University Sports Information.*

Right: Rick Kaminsky set a still-standing Yale record with a 24.9 scoring average as a senior in 1963–64. *Courtesy of Yale University Sports Information.*

with Princeton another time—the Tigers defeated the Elis in a one-game playoff in 1962–63—during his first seven years on the Yale bench.

Vancisin's first Ivy championship team, which came in his debut season of 1956–57, might have been his best. It boasted Johnny Lee, an All-Ivy forward whose likeness adorned the cover of *Sports Illustrated*; nonpareil rebounder Eddie Robinson; and the multi-skilled Larry Downs. Lee averaged 20.2 points per game across three varsity seasons, Downs 19.3. Robinson's spring and determination resulted in 32 rebounds—still the Yale record—one night against Harvard, and he *averaged* 15.6 rebounds for his career.

The brightest moment for this band of Elis may have come in defeat. They gave North Carolina, which went through the season without a defeat en route to winning the NCAA championship, a whale of a game before succumbing in the East Region's opening round. The final score, 90–74, wasn't indicative of the Bulldogs' tenacity and pluck. "That North Carolina team with Lenny Rosenbluth…we stayed with them for thirty-five minutes until we fouled out the first five," Vancisin remembered.

His other Ivy titlist, the 1961–62 squad, was a solid unit that assembled an 18-6 won-lost record. Sophomore Rick Kaminsky—a career 20.1 scorer and a Helms All-American forward as a senior despite his six-one stature—and captain Bill Madden were the stars.

In the NCAA Tournament, this Yale team dropped a 92–82 overtime decision to a potent Wake Forest led by All-American forward Lenny Chappell and a guard named Billy Packer. (Wake was ousted by a Jerry Lucas–John Havlicek–led Ohio State in the Final Four.)

In his later years, though, when the talent at hand diminished and some of his league rivals—Princeton, Penn and even Brown—moved past the Elis, Vancisin frequently came under fire.

His last seven teams were losers, with a 3-20 finish last season being the worst. Attendance at the Payne Whitney decreased at an alarming rate, with gatherings of five hundred and six hundred becoming commonplace. It took a visiting team with a large following, such as UConn or Penn, to pack the place.

Despite these low points, Vancisin would bristle when somebody would call basketball "the stepchild of Yale athletics." "That bothers me," he would say. "It doesn't have to be."

And so it doesn't. Yale deserves better. Joe V. deserved better.

Waterbury Republican, April 27, 1975

VERDERAME RECALLS GLORY YEARS AT WILBUR CROSS

Sal Verderame is eighty-two years old, and he doesn't think he'll be able to attend the Connecticut Sports Writers' Alliance's Gold Key Dinner in Hartford. Sal Verderame will probably spend the day in his apartment at the Josephine Towers on Union Street. "I had a heart attack about a year ago. When it's a cold day, I don't go out much," he said.

The senior Verderame would like to be there for his son. He would like to be seated at a table close to the front of the ballroom at Valle's, close enough so that he can see his son receive a Gold Key from the writers.

This is a prestigious award, and fifty-four-year-old Salvatore "Red" Verderame is a special man. His father is justifiably proud. "His mother

Wilbur Cross Coach Red Verderame, *left*, with his assistant and eventual successor, Bob Saulsbury. Combined, they amassed fourteen state titles and more than 730 wins. *Courtesy of Bob Saulsbury.*

and I were divorced, and I remarried and moved to Waterbury. I've been here about thirty-five years," said the father, a retired salesman of Italian cheese. "I don't see a lot of him, but we have a nice relationship. I'm proud he's done well."

No question Red Verderame has done well. Was there ever a better high school basketball coach in the state? He never seemed to lose when he coached those Wilbur Cross of New Haven teams to state championship after state championship in the late 1950s and early '60s.

Is there a better basketball ambassador to Africa? For nearly twenty years, he has devoted a portion of his summers to teaching Dr. Naismith's game to Africans of many nations under the auspices of the State Department. Hundreds, even thousands, of young men and women on the so-called Dark Continent are able to dribble, pass and shoot basketballs, thanks to this man.

Is there a better vice-principal at Hillhouse High School? Wait...what is he doing at Hillhouse High? "I would have to say that, at first, my being here seems incongruous," said Verderame, who has been vice-principal at Wilbur Cross's arch rival for eleven years. "The first five years here, in my heart, I was pulling for Cross whenever there was a game with Hillhouse. I couldn't help it."

Red Verderame coached Wilbur Cross at a time when high school basketball commanded much of the state's attention. The University of Connecticut was tucked up there someplace, in the northeast corner of the state, and nobody had heard of Fairfield University.

If you wanted to watch basketball, you went to watch the Governors or Hillhouse or Hartford Public. You watched if you could get a ticket. "I was there when it was probably the most exciting. We had super coverage in the newspapers. Full-page coverage with action photos," Verderame said. "They used to televise our games with Hillhouse. We used to play them at the Payne Whitney Gym before three thousand people. You couldn't get a ticket. It was," he said, "the time for high school basketball. It was the peak."

The Verderame era at Wilbur Cross lasted thirteen seasons, from 1953 through '66. His teams won four straight Class L state titles, 1958–61, and another in his final season. There were two New England titles, 1958 and '60, and numerous District League championships.

The Verderame won-lost record reads 236-36. A winning percentage of .868.

"Our 1957–58 team probably was the best," he said. "We went undefeated and beat Somerville, Massachusetts, for the New England title. Don Ferrara and Johnny Coppola were the co-captains. Dom Perno was a junior, and we also had Bill Hulteen and Bobby Melotto. Coppola would start, and then Melotto would come in a few minutes after.

The late Dave Hicks, a six-five All-State center who starred on the last three of Verderame's four straight Wilbur Cross state championship teams (1959–60–61), was regarded as the Governors' greatest player prior to the arrival of John Williamson. Hicks went directly from Cross to the Harlem Globetrotters. *Courtesy of* New Haven Register.

"The '59–60 team was good. We won the New England title with [Dave] Hicks, [Mike] Gore, Melotto, [Phil] Brooks and [Ralph] Buccini. George Jackson was a sophomore. But for teamwork and desire, I would say the '58 team was better."

Hicks, a six-five center with all-around skills, was considered the finest high school player in Connecticut. He eventually landed a spot with the Harlem Globetrotters. Perno, later a fine guard at UConn and now the coach of an undefeated, nationally ranked Husky team, was a superb scholastic player, too.

"Hicks's temperament was excellent. He ranks with Perno," Red said. "Dom had a blowtorch for a heart. He was a skinny six-one, but he played like a kid six-foot-eight, 240."

In his early years at Cross, Verderame was considered an innovator. Sometimes his strategy was panned. Lacking the talent to play Hillhouse or a Public at full tilt, Red perfected the slow-down tactics we see today with North Carolina.

We were doing that in—what?—1955, '56. We were holding the ball then, with a good foul shooter controlling it. They called it the "Deep Freeze" when we beat the Hillhouse "Wonder Five."

I was severely criticized for doing it. That probably was the low point of my coaching career. One writer said I shouldn't be coaching. He misunderstood the tactic. I wanted to hold it until the last three minutes and then play all out. It's like I'm shooting against Rick Barry. If we take two shots, I might beat him. If we take fifty there's no chance.

I got a letter from the coach at San Francisco [Phil Woolpert] when it happened. He said that in coaching, you had to take risks. That just reinforced what I thought.

When New Haven's school boundaries were altered in the mid-1950s, Wilbur Cross began to "get the kids Hillhouse was graced with for years." Then there was no stopping the Governors and Verderame. After Perno and Hicks came Doug Wardlaw and Tony Proto and Glenn Pollard and Alex Scott. They beat Hillhouse eleven straight times, they won forty-six straight games and they invariably defeated some of the good Yale freshman squads.

"We knocked them off three years in a row," Verderame recalled. "In fact, when they had [Rick] Kaminsky and [Denny] Lynch, they won the Ivy League title as sophomores the following year."

Bob Saulsbury, who was Verderame's assistant, has kept Cross at or near the top in succeeding years. He's even surpassed the master in total victories. Red laughs about that.

"We used to kid about it. One time Bob said, 'I'm going to beat your wins tomorrow.' I said, 'That's fine. But you can't beat the won-and-lost percentage.'"

Nobody won with greater frequency than Salvatore "Red" Verderame, and that's one of the reasons why he's being honored by the writers Monday night.

Sal Verderame Sr. may miss the dinner, but he can feel a deep sense of pride just the same.

Waterbury American, January 14, 1981

CHAPTER 4
The Teams

LIONS KING OF THE COURT

NEW BRITAIN—"If we could play together for the next ten years, we'd be the best team in pro basketball."

One could forgive Louie Kinchen, Bassick High's jet-quick point guard, for overstatement. He was caught up in the moment—Bassick's moment of triumph.

On second thought, perhaps Kinchen wasn't exaggerating at all; perhaps this undefeated state championship team of Lions could, in time, enter the NBA en masse and exhibit similar superiority. Certainly their talent and depth is remarkable enough to evoke comparisons with proud high school teams in Connecticut's past—the Warren Hardings and the Hillhouses and the Wilbur Crosses and the Hartford Publics, any and all of the best. Bassick's myriad accomplishments during the 1988–89 season included:

- Twenty-three games without a defeat
- The MBIAC championship
- Its first Class L state championship in fifty years by virtue of last Saturday's 76–72 double-overtime triumph over Harding at Central Connecticut State University's Kaiser Hall
- Three wins over Harding and a home-and-home sweep over number three Hamden and its All-Stater, Scott Burrell
- A number ten ranking in *USA Today*'s national poll

Bassick High senior Angel Echevarria pulls down a rebound against Warren Harding in the 1988–89 Class L state championship game in New Britain. Echevarria later distinguished himself in another sport; he batted a lifetime .280 in baseball's Major Leagues (1996–2002). *Ed Brinsko / Bridgeport Light.*

There are no more hurdles, no more obstacles, no more bridges to cross. The 1988–89 Lions have silenced their few remaining detractors; they are Bridgeport's best, and they are the state's best. The team of tournament MVP Harper Williams (31 points, 14 rebounds) and Jerome Johnson and Angel Echevarria and Louie Kinchen and Cory Smith and Eric Geer is a team to be remembered.

"This was for bragging rights for the summer," said Harrison Taylor, the Lions' head coach, who finally emerged from the shadow cast by his longtime friend and rival, Harding's Charlie Bentley. "I'm tired of looking at Charlie's championship ring. I'm going to get one myself."

The Taylor-Bentley friendship is of some thirty years' duration and has survived their coaching rivalry and Harding's domination. Each was the best man at the other's wedding; each is the godfather for the other's child.

Until this season, Taylor and Bassick were 0-17 against Bentley's Presidents. He endured the taunts and the jibes of being second best, of not being able to win when it counted. Even in triumph, there was a touch of rancor in Taylor's voice when he said, "Because of all the accolades and the big building, people thought we were going to crack. They thought we were going to choke."

No, this Bassick team was not about to mar its splendid season, not with the stakes so high, not before three thousand fans and a WICC radio audience. Victory No. 23 was special, although, as once might suspect, it was difficult to attain.

Harding, competing in the Class L state championship game for a record seventh straight year, actually came within several seconds of winning its sixth title in that span (and tenth overall). With twenty seconds left in regulation, Malcolm Leak's driving layup had pulled the Presidents abreast at 64, and Alex "Boobie" Wright (17 points) tapped in his missed free throw to place Harding in the lead, 66–64.

Malcolm Leak? Well, yes. After missing eleven games with a viral infection, the six-seven senior made a melodramatic return to the Harding lineup, providing both an inspirational lift and 13 points.

His Bassick counterpart, Williams, quickly demonstrated why he is being coveted by dozens of colleges with prestigious basketball programs. With nine seconds left, his jump shot from the baseline rolled around and dropped in, tying the score. Echevarria's forceful rejection of Robert White's driving layup preserved the status quo and sent the game into overtime.

The first three-minute overtime period was scoreless, in part because the underrated Echevarria (13 rebounds) blocked Damon Lewis's game-winning attempt in the final two seconds. "At the end," said Angel, "we had to step up our game to another level of intensity."

Kinchen, whose ability to penetrate and handle the ball under pressure was an important factor throughout the season, took charge in the second overtime by scoring 5 of his 9 points. A 3-point play by the Lions' five-eleven junior—following his interception of a wayward Harding pass—put Bassick ahead to stay, 69–66. And then, after Leak's emphatic jam had pulled the Presidents within two, 74–72, Kinchen hit two free throws, the last with four seconds left.

Bassick's depth was such that it was able to win without a contribution from Johnson, its number two scorer and arguably its finest all-around player. The six-five senior had incurred a hyper-extended knee injury in a practice the previous Monday and sat out the Lions' semifinal victory over Middletown. Taylor made an eleventh-hour decision to place Jerome in the starting lineup but withdrew him in the opening two minutes after deciding "he had no lateral movement."

"We won it for Jerome Johnson," said Kinchen. "By the look in his eyes, I knew he wasn't going to play. The rest of us had to take up the slack."

Another under-publicized player, Cory Smith, was the dominant player when Bassick reeled off 14 unanswered points to begin the second half. Taylor said: "We had been grooming him for two or three years to shoot the 3-pointer." The six-four senior contributed 9 points during that spurt and 12 of his 19 in the quarter, which ended with the Lions holding a seemingly secure 58–42 lead.

Of course, no advantage is safe against Harding. Too much talent, too much tradition. A combination of the Presidents' pressing defense and some questionable Bassick shots transformed an apparent rout into a nail-biter. Harding opened the final period by scoring 13 straight points, and suddenly it was 58–55.

Williams ended that streak by depositing a rebound, hitting the floor as the ball dropped through the cords. But the Presidents' surge continued, and they tied the score at 62 when Lewis (15 points) converted the first of a one-and-one. He made the second, too, but it was disallowed because of a lane violation.

Warren Harding Coach Charlie Bentley was gracious in defeat, even joining his friend, Bassick Coach Harrison Taylor, for a post-game photo following the Lions' double-overtime victory in the state title game. *Ed Brinsko* / Bridgeport Light.

A layup by Williams restored order momentarily, before Leak and Wright parlayed their talents to give Harding its final lead at 66–64.

Bentley was gracious in defeat. The Harding coach extended congratulations to Taylor and Bassick and spoke with pride about his own fine team. "After all the preseason workouts, after what happened in New Jersey [a 67–28 blowout by St. Anthony's, the nation's number one team], the guys dug down. I'm proud of them," he said.

Harrison Taylor and his assistant, Bernie Lofton, were issuing similar statements. And in the crowd, a man named Bud Knittel, who had coached Bassick into the state semifinals in the mid-1970s, smiled. "He gave me my start," Taylor noted. "I owe a lot to him."

Bridgeport Light, March 22, 1989

THE WATERBURY CONNECTION DELIVERS

SPRINGFIELD, Massachusetts—It was considerably more than a pickup game at the Orange Street playground, but some of the faces were the same.

There, on one side, were Tony Hanson, springy and intense, and Jim Abromaitis, tall and blond. On the other side was an angular black youth named Bill Eason, firing in jump shots with consummate ease.

The Hanson-Eason rivalry, in particular, goes back a long way and built to a peak during their scholastic days at Holy Cross and Kennedy, respectively. Each had a following claiming their man was the more gifted player.

On Saturday, the Hanson camp was in position to speak the loudest.

The University of Connecticut, with Messrs. Hanson and Abromaitis playing major supporting roles behind a five-ten dynamo named Joe Whelton, stunned the Northeast portion of the civilized world by overturning Providence, 87–73, for the ECAC New England Championship before 8,775 people at the Springfield Civic Center. The Friars' Eason, shackled by early fouls, wasn't much of a factor.

Stunned, of course, is the correct word. Few gave the Huskies a chance of surviving Thursday night's opening-round game against Massachusetts, never mind reaching the ECAC New England title game opposite Providence and advancing to their first NCAA Tournament since 1967.

"Two weeks ago, after we lost to New Hampshire in overtime, this was probably the furthest thing from my mind," admitted Abromaitis, who contributed eight points and five rebounds to UConn's eighteenth triumph of the year.

"Beating Providence has got to give us some confidence because they've beaten some good teams," added the six-seven freshman, who proceeded to reel off the names of the more prominent Friar victims…Louisville, St. John's, Oregon.

An incident—an unfortunate incident, said the more charitable—in the second half played a role in the Connecticut victory. Just how large nobody will ever know. The Huskies' lead, once an awesome eighteen points, had dwindled to eight when, during a Connecticut in-bounds, the Friars' Steve Strother sent Whelton to the floor (one is tempted to say canvas)

Joe Whelton, clever point guard and MVP of the 1975–76 ECAC New England Tournament, lays up a two-pointer. *Courtesy of University of Connecticut Athletic Communications.*

with an elbow or forearm. Whelton, the Huskies' floor leader who had accounted for 14 points at this juncture, did not immediately get up.

Those who had witnessed Joe Hassett's elbow-swinging incident Thursday night, when he knocked Holy Cross's Leo Kane out of their first-round game, suddenly asked themselves: does Providence play dirty basketball?

"I don't want to attack Providence as a team," said Hanson with emotion, "but both incidents were very uncalled for. More than anything, it could have gone overboard," he continued. "It used to be a way to take a player out of a game. It was a way to throw us off."

It was, Tony Hanson decided, "a very big point" in Saturday's game. "Joey didn't want to go out and fight. He wanted to beat them, and he beat them the way a great player does. He carried our team. What more can you ask of the man?"

Very little. Shortly thereafter, Joe Whelton returned to the floor and, for the remaining ten minutes, played Most Valuable Player basketball. He scored 11 more points—giving the diminutive sophomore 25 for the afternoon—and revived the Connecticut fast break that had been so devastating in the game's opening minutes.

The Huskies won their biggest game of the 1975–76 season going away, and Joseph A. Whelton, former East Catholic High All-Stater, was chosen MVP by the assembled news media.

If Hanson wasn't the scoring leader, as he was on sixteen occasions this season, the curly-haired junior was making other contributions, such as 11 rebounds, including five at the offensive end of the court, and eight assists. Neither figure was surpassed by others on this day.

And if his 16 points, built on 8-for-14 shooting, were slightly below par, it should be remembered that he in large measure was responsible for the Huskies' 37–19 getaway, scoring 12 points during this span. Hanson, like Whelton, was voted to the all-tournament team.

It was a less productive afternoon for Eason, the six-five Providence sophomore who developed his court skills at Kennedy High. Billy had three personal fouls before the game was three minutes old and wound up sitting much of the time. The region's third most accurate percentage shooter (57 percent for the year) finished with a subpar 3-for-11 and eight points.

Still, there may be more to come for all concerned. While Hanson, Abromaitis, Whelton & Co. goes off to Providence for the NCAA Eastern Regionals, PC stands a strong chance of getting a return trip to the National Invitation Tournament.

"I know we're peaking," added Abromaitis, whose nineteenth birthday today should be even more festive, "but I hope we haven't finished peaking."

Waterbury Sunday Republican, March 7, 1976

TORRID-SHOOTING FAIRFIELD SOARS TO TOP IN EAST

FAIRFIELD, Connecticut—On the fifth day of February, Fred Barakat awoke to discover that Fairfield University had the best won-lost record in New England.

Yes, better than Providence. Better than Holy Cross. Better than any other eastern college classified as Division I by the NCAA.

Nationally ranked Providence had lost—at home—to Villanova on January 31, and now the Stags, at 17-2, had the highest winning percentage in the region.

Surprised? Not any more than Barakat, the self-proclaimed street kid from Union City, New Jersey, who coaches Fairfield.

"I'm elated that the team has responded so well," he said, "but I honestly didn't think our record would be so lofty at this stage. We're not saying we're great. We're in the midst of something nice that's happening to us."

Fairfield, a small (enrollment 2,600) Catholic college where academics take priority over jump shots, isn't supposed to be challenging Providence, Georgetown and the rest for eastern supremacy, but the Stags are doing it. Their style of play—a running game with control—produces points in bunches and pleases the crowds. Remarkably, the Stags are guilty of few turnovers, despite a per-game scoring average of 90.1, which ranks seventh in the nation.

On the morning of January 22, New Englanders were jarred into consciousness when they read the following score in their Sunday newspaper: Fairfield 123, Holy Cross 103. This game, above all others, proved to the Stags' detractors that they were for real.

"This could be the finest win we've ever had because of who we were playing," pointed out Barakat, who felt the only thing comparable was Fairfield's 80–76 upset win over Marshall in the 1973 National Invitation Tournament.

"We were totally prepared for them, as prepared as we'll ever be or have been prepared for anyone," he added. "I thought we could win, but we certainly didn't anticipate beating them like this."

The Stags, shooting 64 percent (41 for 65) from the field and sinking 41 of 50 foul shots, nearly ran the then-fourteenth-in-the-nation Crusaders out of Fairfield's campus gym. The 123 points represented three highs: most points scored by Fairfield, most points scored against Holy Cross and most points scored in the Stags' gym.

A word of caution about this gymnasium, where virtually all of the 3,200 in attendance appear to be sitting within inches of the court: as far as the NCAA Statistics Service can determine, the 26-game home court winning streak Fairfield carried into February 5 represented the longest still intact in the nation. Should one wish to delve further into the past, he will discover the Stags own a 64-7 record there over the last six years.

Three seniors, two juniors and a sophomore, holdovers all, have made the Stags jell. Road losses to improved Boston College (79–76) and South Carolina (75–69) are the only blemishes on an otherwise perfect season.

Barakat, in his eighth year at Fairfield after serving as an assistant at Connecticut and Assumption, his alma mater, said, "Their attitude is the intangible that just doesn't allow time to get depressed in crucial situations."

Fairfield partisans and others regard Joe DeSantis, a curly-haired junior who was an all–New York City scholastic player at St. Nicholas of Tolentine, as the premier guard in New England, a latter-day version of Providence's unflappable Ernie DiGregorio. Ernie D. Joey D.

The numbers and the eye say this is so. All–New England and honorable mention All-America as a sophomore, the six-two DeSantis has been ever better this season, averaging 21.8 points and seven assists. He is without peer as a passer, and his long-range jump shots have produced games of 38, 36 and 32 points.

"It was a little too much DeSantis," said Lou Rossini, the veteran St. Francis of New York coach, after a 29-point, 12-assist, six-rebound performance by Joey D. toppled the resurgent Terriers, 96–87.

One DeSantis play that night—a between-the-legs bounce pass to Kim Fisher that resulted in an unmolested two-pointer—brought down the house.

Fisher, a six-one senior whose previous claim to fame was an aunt, Gail Fisher, who co-starred on the television series

Junior guard Joe DeSantis scores in front of Holy Cross's Ronnie Perry during the Stags' 123–103 triumph over the then-nationally ranked Crusaders on January 21, 1978. *Tom Kabelka / courtesy* Waterbury Republican-American.

The face of New England college basketball, circa 1978: Fairfield Coach Fred Barakat is interviewed by Bob Cousy at courtside in the Providence Civic Center as PC Coach Dave Gavitt listens in. *Joseph Sia / courtesy of Fairfield University Sports Information.*

Mannix, has achieved stardom himself. "Silk" is what they call the youngster who burned Holy Cross for 28 points and averages eighteen.

"He's one of the best guards in the East, and nobody knows it," DeSantis said of his backcourt partner.

Barakat goes a step further. "DeSantis is a better total player than DiGregorio at a similar stage in their careers. Fisher is as good as any guard in the East. Our combination of guards is as good as anybody's," he declared.

There is ample size up front, especially when Mark Plefka, a six-nine senior from East Hartford, comes off the bench to join six-ten Mark Young and six-eight senior Steve Balkun. Young, a muscular, 240-pounder who was a scholastic All-America in Brookline, Massachusetts, is sinking better than 63 percent of his shots and averaging 15.3 points. Brendan Suhr, the Stags' associate coach, says he's "the best center in New England."

Balkun has taken his captain's role seriously. Although a 58.8 percent marksman, the quiet youngster from West Hartford's Northwest Catholic High willingly passes up shots to concentrate on defense and rebounding. In the latter area, his 10.7 average leads the region.

"There has been a tremendous commitment by our captain to accept a role most kids wouldn't accept, especially in their senior year," Barakat said in noting Balkun's unselfishness.

Still, Balkun has averaged 10.3 points, slightly behind sophomore Jerome "Flip" Williams, the Stags' small forward, who has a 10.7 norm.

Plefka, who contributes 9.4 points per game, reached a personal high of 24 in the landmark win over Holy Cross.

Why has Fairfield improved so much from last year's team that went 16-9 and then dropped a pair of games in the Eastern College Athletic Conference New England Regional? Some of the answers—experience, maturity, "improvement in every kid"— are expected. One was not.

"We go to church together, at home and on the road," said Barakat, who never would have been confused with Oral Roberts in the past. Indeed, Fred Barakat, thirty-eight-year-old former street kid, has become a new man, a calmer man, a man less apt to lash out at those he considers his enemies. Coach and players have matured together.

"When we played at South Carolina, we called a Methodist minister and asked him to open his church for fifteen minutes," he said. "When we played at Canisius, we called a security guard to open the chapel. We don't pray to win; we just pray to be free of injury."

Another man in the Fairfield hierarchy, Athletic Director Don Cook, has been turning to prayer more often these days, too. The demand for tickets—by alumni, students, townies—has far exceeded the supply, and his nerves are being tested.

The Cook telephone rings unceasingly; he's been stopped on the street by strangers and even approached at social gatherings. One man was brazen enough to call the Cook home on Christmas morning, proclaiming himself both a relative of the university president and an alumnus, and requested two tickets for the Holy Cross game.

"I don't care if you were born in a manger," Cook replied before returning the receiver to its cradle.

Sporting News, February 18, 1978

SEIRUP'S TIGERS ROARED TO NEW ENGLAND TITLE

We can thank a venerable group known as the Greater Bridgeport Old Timers Athletic Association for bringing attention to the fortieth anniversary of Roger Ludlowe's New England high school basketball championship.

On May 8, the old-timers presented the George Sherwood Award to Bob Seirup at their thirty-eighth annual banquet. Seirup's contributions to area athletics ran the gamut from athlete and coach to official and referee, but his greatest accomplishment was coaching Roger Ludlowe High School to the 1954–55 New England title—the first and only by a Fairfield school. Only two other Fairfield County high schools, Bridgeport Central (1950 and 1934) and Bassick (1940), were to claim the regional championship prior to the death of the New Englands in the early 1960s.

These days, Seirup, sixty-eight, may be found on Lawrence Road, in the pleasant Cape Cod–style home he shares with Joan, his wife of forty-five years. Their three children have grown up and moved on, and now the family circle has widened to embrace five grandchildren.

He is virtually retired now, except for an occasional stint in real estate or property management work. More than fourteen years have elapsed since he taught physical education in the Fairfield school system, and nearly thirty-five years have passed since he left coaching—which was an unpaid assignment in that era—in favor of officiating.

The lone reminder of Ludlowe's singular achievement at Boston Garden in March 1955 may be found on a shelf in the Seirup living room. It's a game ball that bears the names of the opponents and scores from the Tigers' progression to the New England title:

- Ludlowe 76, Manchester (New Hampshire) Central 59
- Ludlowe 58, Bangor, Maine 52
- Ludlowe 62, Somerville, Massachusetts 58

"We had a good team, but when you hit tournament play, it's the breaks," Seirup said of his alma mater's first and only trip to the New England Tournament. "I think the whole town was there for the championship. You didn't know you had that many people with you."

Layton Davis Coombs Jr., who answered to "Dave" or "Rebel," was the team's captain and star, a six-one senior who was considered the state's finest college prospect. He would average nearly twenty-five points per game that winter, earning All-State and All-New England recognition and a basketball scholarship to the University of West Virginia. No surprise there. Coombs spent most of his formative years in Morgantown, home of the state university, before his family arrived in Fairfield.

Recalled Seirup: "The Celtics came out and checked our kid with the two-handed jump shot. That was Coombs."

Coombs shared the Roger Ludlowe starting lineup with two other seniors: Lee Linderman, an angular six-five forward, and Bob Gillette,

Coach Bob Seirup is hoisted aloft by his Roger Ludlowe players after winning the 1954–55 New England Interscholastic championship at Boston Garden. *Courtesy of Joan Seirup.*

a diminutive guard and class president. The center was Dave Graham, a powerfully built six-four junior who would earn All-State recognition in back-to-back seasons—in football—and later play offensive tackle for the Philadelphia Eagles. Junior Dave Potts was the other guard for the Tigers until being supplanted by Harry Hyra in the state tournament. Hyra, a wiry junior, made the most of the opportunity. He averaged a complementary 17 points in four state tournament games (behind Coombs's 19.5) and 15.3 in the New Englands. Coombs scored a tournament-record 80 points in the three games at Boston Garden.

"Hyra made [second-team] All-State and All-New England, yet never started a game until the state tournament," Seirup said. "What a sixth man he was." And what a father. Most people know his daughter these days as the actress Meg Ryan.

Ludlowe encountered few figurative potholes on its route to Boston. There was an early loss to Stamford and another later to Warren Harding. In mid-February, the sharp-shooting Coombs set a school record with 43

Coach Bob Seirup with the nucleus of the 1954–55 championship team, *from left*: Bob Gillette, Dave Potts, Dave Graham, Lee Linderman, Dave Coombs and Harry Hyra. *Courtesy of Joan Seirup.*

points in a 79–40 rout of Bullard-Havens. The Tigers entered the Class L state tournament with a 16-2 record and a number two seeding.

As expected, Seirup's finest team experienced little trouble in the tournament, breezing past Hall of West Hartford, Hartford Public and Stratford en route to its meeting with undefeated, top-ranked Hillhouse in the old New Haven Arena. The Fairfield school led early, but the fabled "Wonder Five," with all five starters averaging double figures, pulled away for a 61–47 victory. "We're going to Boston!" chanted fans from both sides. Dave Coombs, who scored 22 points in the championship game, was voted Most Valuable Player.

Said Seirup: "Everyone raved about the Wonder Five. I always felt we were better, although we weren't the night we played them." He pauses. "Maybe that loss helped us when we got to Boston."

Gillette, an erudite man who has taught English in the Fairfield high schools for a quarter century, looks back with fondness on the

Tigers' experiences in Boston Garden. "We were just awe-struck by the phenomenon," he said. "It was as if the entire school was there, and half of the town."

During a practice, Gillette received some advice from a well-dressed man about a dead spot on the Garden's parquet floor. "Do you know who that was?" a Ludlowe coach said. Gillette had failed to recognize the Celtics' Bob Cousy.

Roger Ludlowe couldn't have been too awed by the Garden or the capacity crowds of thirteen thousand. The Tigers played some of their most inspired basketball as they whipped Central of Manchester—Coombs connected on a sixty-footer to end the third quarter en route to a 34-point evening—and squeaked past Bangor in the semifinals. Hillhouse should have been waiting in the championship game, but Somerville upset the Academics, 67–65, in the other semifinal.

Ludlowe upheld Connecticut's prestige by coming from behind in the fourth quarter to defeat Somerville, 62–58, for the New England title.

Most of the champion Tigers gathered for their fiftieth reunion in 2005. *Front row, from left*: Manager Joe Noga, Harry Hyra, Dave Potts, Bob Gillette. *Standing*: Assistant Coach Fern Tetreau, Peter Brown, Roger Soderholm, Lee Linderman, Dave Graham, Coach Bob Seirup. *Courtesy of Joan Seirup.*

Remarkably, all of the Tigers' 12 points in the final period resulted from free throws. Between them, Coombs and Hyra accounted for 41 points.

The post-game celebration in Boston Garden was just the beginning. "When our train arrived in Fairfield the next day, the station was blanketed with people," Gillette recalled. Official crowd estimates ranged from eight thousand to ten thousand. "They held ceremonies at trackside, and then they marched us onto a flatbed truck for a parade. It was similar to what they captured in *Hoosiers*."

Seirup is pleased that so many of the players on this celebrated team have done well in life. Graham went on to the University of Virginia, where he captained the football team, and then played four NFL seasons with Philadelphia. Today, he's a middle school principal in Marshall, Virginia.

"I don't think we knew how good we were going to be," Graham said from his Virginia home. "I was a rebounder, a football player playing basketball. We had nice balance to go with the shooters we had."

Both Gillette and Potts earned degrees from Wesleyan. Hyra and Linderman captained their respective teams at Fairfield and Amherst. Dick Dirgins, a valuable substitute on the championship team, graduated from Norwich and became a U.S. Army brigadier general. He died this winter at fifty-seven.

Coombs? There are conflicting stories. Seirup and Gillette agree that he played freshman basketball at West Virginia and then dropped out of school. (He averaged 24.0 points a game with the Mountaineer frosh.) After serving with the Eighty-second Airborne Division, Rebel enrolled at High Point College in North Carolina and played on the varsity in the 1959–60 season. He averaged 18.9 points but appeared in just eight of the team's twenty-three games.

After that? Nobody seems to know for certain.

Fairfield Citizen-News, May 26, 1995

CHAMPIONS...THEN AND ALWAYS

The team was undersized and, starter for starter, perhaps less talented than a couple of its Sacred Heart University predecessors. But the 1985–86 Pioneers exceeded the sum of their parts and left an unforgettable legacy—the first NCAA Division II national basketball title won by a New England school.

Before a vociferous crowd of 5,863 in the Springfield Civic Center, Sacred Heart defeated Southeast Missouri State, 93–87, in the 1986 championship game, capping a remarkable 30-4 season. Coach Dave Bike was voted National Coach of the Year, senior co-captain Roger Younger was selected a first-team All-American and several of his teammates won lesser honors.

Dave Bike coached Sacred Heart's 1985–86 team to the NCAA Division II national title—the first by a New England institution. *Courtesy of Sacred Heart University Athletic Communications.*

On Alumni Day, February 17, members of the championship team, including Bike and assistant coaches Bobby Jenkins and Adolph Ellis, will receive a well-deserved tenth anniversary tribute prior to—and following—the men's game against New Hampshire College.

But let's not wait. Here are recollections from many of the men who made the national title a reality. In their own words:

JOE JACKSON: As a co-captain, the effervescent Jackson was the squad's invaluable "sixth man," the player who ignited a spark upon entering a game. His contributions—7.7 points, 4.5 rebounds and incalculable amounts of hustle—complemented the well-rounded starting five. Jackson is in his eighth year as a patrol officer with the Ansonia Police Department.

Co-captain Joe Jackson celebrates Sacred Heart's NCAA national title. *Courtesy of Sacred Heart University Athletic Communications.*

In practice before the season, I came up with a slogan: "We're on a mission." We used that the entire year.

Coach Bike asked me if I wanted to start and I told him "no." It's all about who finishes.

The last home game I told the crowd I was going to dunk. I'd never dunked before in a game. When I did, the place went crazy—except for Coach Bike.

In the tournament, one of our biggest scares came against Florida Southern in the semifinals. If Keith Johnson didn't make a basket just before halftime, we would have been down by ten points. His play gave us the momentum we needed for the second half.

ROGER YOUNGER: Many people regard Younger as the university's finest all-around guard. As senior co-captain, the man from Middletown was a first-team All-American in the championship season, the team's leading scorer (18.9), free-throw shooter (.828) and passer (181 assists) and, fittingly, MVP of the championship tournament. Two telling statistics of Younger's unparalleled capacity for winning: three New England

Roger Younger, MVP of the 1985–86 NCAA Division II national tournament, works his magic against Quinnipiac. *Courtesy of Sacred Heart University Athletic Communications.*

Regional titles and a composite 108-23 record in his four seasons as a starter. He went on to the Boston Celtics' rookie camp and later played professionally in Yugoslavia.

The team I played with as a freshman had what I consider three All-Americans— Keith Bennett, Rhonie Wright and Herb Camero—and a true point guard, Steve Zazuri. That team would have beaten my senior team.

My senior year, we had no point guard and everyone [up front] was a small forward. But we were hard to match up against and talented across the board. Travis Smith was more talented than anyone on the team, but he held himself back.

Without question, winning the national championship was an unreal experience. With about nineteen, twenty seconds left in the championship game, I looked at Kevin Stevens and said, "I'm about to faint. This is unbelievable."

KEITH JOHNSON: At six-four, Johnson often gave up several inches to opposing centers, but he surrendered none of the area within the paint. Alternating between center and forward, he led the squad in rebounding (8.2) and blocked shots (49) and ranked second in scoring (15.8). The junior from West Haven registered a game-high 22 points in the national semifinal win over Florida Southern and earned a berth on the all-tournament team. He's employed by Turbine Components of Branford.

I was a freshman in 1982–83 when we had Bennett, Wright, Camero and Zazuri, and that was probably our best team, although we lost in the national quarterfinals.

We faced a lot of good big men in our championship season. Cleveland Woods of New Hampshire College was versatile, Norman Taylor of UB, Ivan Olivares of Springfield.

When we played at Norfolk State in the quarterfinals, we got pumped up when they told us we shouldn't have bothered to show up. Their big gun, Ralph Talley, had an off game and we won [84–74].

TRAVIS SMITH: A fine all-around player who, at six-four, was a tall junior guard in the championship season, he averaged 14.6 points and 4.5 assists and led the team with 81 steals. He recorded a triple double (17 points,

13 rebounds, 10 assists) in the semifinal victory over Florida Southern. Smith played two years of professional basketball in Chile and one season in the CBA. He's now the recreation coordinator for the Youth Confinement Center in New Haven.

Going into the season, I thought we were good enough to win the regional. After we achieved that goal, we said, "Let's keep going."

Everybody that we played in the tournament was good. The team that should have beaten us was Springfield in the regional semifinals. We were down with fifteen seconds left in regulation, as I recall, but Roger [Younger] tied the game and we won it in—what?—double overtime. Southeast Missouri was pretty good, but I think they gave up in the stretch.

KEVIN STEVENS: The Pioneers' power forward, Stevens was a six-five junior capable of outscrapping taller opponents. Despite a dislocated left ankle that kept him out of eight games, he averaged 14.5 points and 7.8 rebounds and topped the team with a 58.9 field goal percentage. In the championship game, Stevens's 19 points led six Pioneers in double figures. He recently married Nancy Orman and is working in sales at Total Communications in Fairfield.

I remember giving Joe Jackson, one of our co-captains, a ride home and he predicted it would be our year.

Before I got hurt, I was playing as well as I had in my whole life. When I dislocated the ankle against New Haven in late January, I thought I was done for the year. But I really worked hard to come back for the league playoffs. When I rejoined the team, half the time I came off the bench. But I started in the national semis and finals.

Indicative of how well the team played was our balanced scoring. All

Kevin Stevens, with 19 points, topped six Pioneers in double figures in the title game victory. *Courtesy of Sacred Heart University Athletic Communications.*

of the starters averaged double figures. I think some of Sacred Heart's earlier teams overwhelmed people with their talent. We had a knack for winning.

I don't think we were favored in the championship game. No New England team had won the Division II national championship. Southeast Missouri was a large state school with an undergraduate population of thirteen thousand. We had maybe seventeen hundred. But we'd come from behind to beat Florida Southern in the semifinals, and we knew we had a chance.

TONY JUDKINS: As a six-five freshman, Judkins met the pressure of a national championship season head-on. Thrust into the starting lineup at the outset, he averaged 10.3 points and rebounded aggressively across thirty-four games. As a mature junior and senior, he served as captain and earned All-American honors. People still talk about his off-balance thirty-foot shot at the buzzer that stunned Bridgeport, 69–67, in the 1989 New England Regional finale. Today, he's a planning analyst with the Connecticut Department of Social Services in his native Hartford.

Two weeks before the first game, Coach Bike told me I'd be starting. Those other four guys made it easy to fit in. All I had to do was get open and spot up.

In the playoffs, my best game probably was against Norfolk State in the national quarterfinals. I was nervous going into a hostile environment and reading about how big they were. I think they were better than Southeast Missouri. But I hit a couple of shots early, and we won.

KEITH GATLING: An angular six-six freshman forward, Gatling found himself in the starting lineup late in the season after Stevens went down with an ankle injury. He was an important role player in NCAA New England Regional victories over Springfield (76–74 in double overtime) and New Hampshire College (83–67). He's now an investigator with the Connecticut Department of Social Services in Bridgeport.

Even as a freshman, I was never really scared. There was nobody tougher than the guys on our team.

I liked the way I played in the regionals against Springfield and New Hampshire. I think everyone was up for the latter game. It was personal; we had lost to them twice during the season.

It wasn't until later, when we came close in our senior year, that Tony [Judkins] and I realized how hard it is to win a national championship.

HOWIE WHITE: A backcourt sparkplug, White appeared in nineteen games in support of Younger and Smith. Today, he's executive director of the Chester Addison Community Center in Stamford.

After our intra-squad scrimmage before the season, I got up in front of everyone and predicted we were going to win everything.

Basically, my job was to pick up the slack defensively, get the ball into the big guys. Everything we did was together. That togetherness was very important. We had the continuity.

Southeast Missouri was bigger than we were, and they came in cocky. They would look at us and laugh. That gave us the extra incentive to win.

Sacred Heart magazine, Winter 1996

WILBUR CROSS THE GREATEST EVER?

STORRS—A lot of people have been asking the question. Neither Bob Saulsbury nor Red Verderame will provide a satisfactory answer.

Is the 1971–72 Wilbur Cross High School team that defeated Hartford Public, 83–77, on Saturday for the Connecticut Interscholastic Athletic Conference Class LL state title more talented than the earlier Cross and Hillhouse juggernauts that are generally considered the finest the state has produced?

"It's not a fair comparison," said Saulsbury, accepting congratulatory handshakes from well-wishers, after coaching the 24-0 Governors to their third state championship in six seasons. "Red played a different type of game. We freelance. We like to throw the ball the length of the court. They played a slower game."

Saulsbury's predecessor, Salvatore "Red" Verderame, who led Wilbur Cross to five state titles and two New England scholastic championships

Coach Bob Saulsbury, *right*, with the co-captains of his second Wilbur Cross High team, Clint Davis, *second from left*, and Alex Scott. At left is Assistant Coach Sal Savo. The Governors won the 1967–68 Class LL state title, and both Davis and Scott were selected to the All-State team. *Courtesy of Bob Saulsbury*.

during his thirteen seasons at the helm, was slightly more forthcoming. "These kids mimic the pros. They pick up all the moves from watching television, which didn't carry as many games then," he said. "It's a hard comparison, really. We played a control game."

Messrs. Saulsbury and Verderame were in agreement on one count, though. "These kids have all the shots," enthused Verderame. "They're a great offensive team, the greatest I've coached," Saulsbury said.

Let's bring an impartial observer into this discussion. Me. I saw the state championship Hillhouse "Wonder Five" of 1954–55 (remember the names? Sal DiNicola, Leon Nelson, Johnny Woods, Gene Davins, Don Perrelli) and the New England championship Cross team of 1959–60 (the incomparable Dave Hicks, Bobby Melotto, Phil Brooks, Ralph Buccini, Mike Gore). This group of Governors is superior.

I missed Hillhouse's undefeated "Fabulous Five" of 1964–65 (Walt Esdaile, Billy Evans, Tom Chapman, Billy Gray, Tony Barone), but I sincerely doubt they would beat this season's Cross squad.

They're bigger, stronger, faster and better shooters. There's not a weak link anywhere. Seniors Mickey Heard (six-three) and Roland Jones (six-four) were selected to the All-State team last year and undoubtedly will be repeaters. They're the co-captains, the stars.

But sophomores Bruce "Soup" Campbell, an angular six-eight, and Jimmy Williamson, a five-ten dynamo, often are more impressive than the upperclassmen, and another starter, six-two senior George Powell, would be the dominant player on many other teams.

Examine the scoring averages they took into Saturday's championship game at the Field House: Jones, 24.3 points per game; Williamson, 19.1; Heard, 18.1; Campbell, 16.2; Powell, 14.6. If you're adding, that's 92 points plus per game. Including the supporting cast, the 1971–72 Governors averaged a record 100 points per contest.

Saulsbury rates Heard the best of the five and the finest player he's ever coached—schoolboy All-American John Williamson, older brother of Jimmy, notwithstanding. "You tell me who's a better ballplayer under pressure," the Cross coach said rhetorically.

Nobody, apparently. Heard's 26-point (ten of nineteen from the field), 10-rebound performance in the title game, which earned him the tournament's Most Valuable Player award, convinced any remaining

Saulsbury taught basketball to this group of youngsters in Mali, West Africa, during the summer of 1969. The boys played the game barefoot. *Courtesy of Bob Saulsbury.*

skeptics among the three thousand in attendance or in the statewide television audience.

Saulsbury, a forty-two-year-old New Haven native, is building an imposing coaching record. His six years at the helm have produced a 126-17 won-lost record, three state titles and five District League championships. He attributes his success to having "good players, luck and good people to work with," the latter a reference to assistant coach Sal Savo.

Bob undoubtedly learned his lessons well, first as a player on Hillhouse's three successive state championship teams (1946, 1947, 1948) coached by Sam Bender and then as an assistant, for six seasons, under Verderame.

When Red resigned following the 1965–66 season to coach and teach basketball in Africa under the auspices of the State Department, he immediately recommended Saulsbury as his successor. The two men remain close friends to this day, even though Red is now the vice-principal at Hillhouse. As Bob puts it, "We still consider Red part of Wilbur Cross."

The "we" is correct. Verderame was standing on the sidelines, under a basket, watching the Cross team and its supporters celebrate, when Heard and Jones walked over and presented him the game ball.

Waterbury Sunday Republican, March 12, 1972

UPDATE: Bob Saulsbury retired from coaching following the 1993–94 season, after 497 victories and 9 state championships. Bruce Campbell and Jimmy "Jiggy" Williamson co-captained his 1973–74 Governor squad, which swept all twenty-four opponents—including a pair of wins over traditional New York City power DeWitt Clinton—en route to a third straight state title and tops-in-the-nation ranking by the *Washington Post*.

CHAPTER 5

Ray Andrade
THE DEVIL DRIVES

T he applause in Ray Andrade's tumultuous life was limited to a handful of months in the winter of 1969–1970, when he captivated a city with his basketball skills. As a seventeen-year-old sophomore guard with silky smooth moves, Andrade directed Bridgeport's Central High School to twenty-three straight victories and a berth in the Class LL state championship game.

He never heard a final round of derisive applause. On an unusually warm Monday evening in January 1992, a small group of people standing on the sidewalk cheered when Andrade's covered body was carried from a small grocery store in Bridgeport's North End, after he was fatally shot by the owner in a botched robbery attempt. "You got what was coming to you!" many shouted.

Few people, even those who were close to Raymond Clifton "Pudgy" (pronounced "Poodgie") Andrade during his thirty-nine years on Earth, were in a position to disagree.

Tom Penders has come a long way from his days at Central High School when he coached Ray Andrade for that one season; he is now the head basketball coach at the University of Texas. He remembers Andrade well. "This was a tragedy," Penders says. "He was one of those kids who couldn't be helped. He could be the most charming person, a leader on the court. He had the ability to play in college and probably be a professional player. That's what makes it so frustrating."

Ray Andrade

A troubled home life coupled with an early addiction to heroin placed Andrade on a path to self-destruction, limiting him to that one memorable season of organized competition and a scholastic record virtually barren of passing grades.

While members of his high school class were preparing for graduation and the next major step in their lives, he was already behind bars for drug-related offenses. He would spend some fifteen years incarcerated, encompassing reformatories, federal and state penitentiaries, for armed bank robbery and other crimes.

New York City's Earl Manigault might be the best known of the playground athletes who succumbed to the lure of the streets, but Ray Andrade's case is similarly tragic in its wasted potential.

THEY TRIED TO HELP

"I cried for three days when I'd heard what happened, but I wasn't shocked [by his death]," says Ernest Parker, a man of compassion who served as both a father figure and big brother to Andrade during a relationship that spanned a quarter century. "He liked the glory that went with basketball, but he lacked the discipline."

Others who were close, or those who knew him from a safer distance, describe a tormented man with a split personality. "Pudgy lived in two worlds," says Kenny Sumpter, perhaps Ray's closest friend, who was the Hilltoppers' team manager during the unforgettable 1969–70 season. "One was basketball, the other was the fast lane. What happened was inevitable."

George Thompson, who played for city rival Bassick before advancing to Southern Illinois and then a successful career in sales management, respected Ray the player but preferred to keep his distance when they dated girls who were close friends. "He had a 'Jekyll and Hyde' personality. I didn't hang around with Ray because he was involved with types of deviant behavior even then," Thompson says.

Now a part-time minister at the Church on the Rock, Thompson uses Ray Andrade in his teachings, especially when he addresses prison inmates. "The guy had one of the best hearts you wanted in a body. But what was on his shoulders was psychopathic and schizophrenic. They never came into unity."

149

Ray Andrade drives against Wilbur Cross in the 1970 Class LL semifinal game won by Central, 105–103. *Central High School* 1970 Criterion *yearbook.*

Regret over Andrade's passing seems proportional to one's appreciation of his basketball skills. "There was a side of him that was so magnetic," says Barry McLeod, among the legion of high school players who was influenced by Andrade's behind-the-back, between-the-legs ball handling and lightning moves to the basket. "I knew he was something special [in basketball], even at the Boys Club. It was incredible what he did in one year at Central."

For an instant, the words end. "I guess," McLeod finally continues, "he had a split personality. He really wasn't a productive member of society at this point. But I hate to see the kid go out like this. It's a shame it had to end this way."

If the words of friends, teachers, coaches and even basketball rivals have any credence, Ray Andrade's positive contributions to society may have been limited to basketball and, near the end, during the months of apparent rehabilitation following his release from prison. Through his job at the University School, a small, private "alternative" high school, and with the Bagley-Walden Foundation, he had counseled kids on the perils of drugs before his life went awry one final time.

"Officially, he wasn't a counselor here, but he talked to the kids and was a positive role image. He was a guy who was there and was looking to come back into society," says Nicholas Macol, the school's director.

In the spring, Macol considered Andrade an asset, but when the former sports star returned in the fall, Macol says he hardly recognized Andrade; he seemed totally debilitated, a wasted shadow. By November, he was forced to dismiss Andrade because "his whole personality and chemistry were destroyed."

BRIGHT MOMENTS

In a city renowned for its basketball, Ray Andrade is a playground legend. He should have been a Bridgeport high school legend and more. For an all-too-brief period, he was right up there with Porky Vieira, Ron DelBianco, Jack Kvancz and Dave Bike, who preceded him; Central teammate Rich Semo; his peers, Walter Luckett, Frank Oleynick and McLeod; and those who would follow: Wes Matthews, John Bagley, John Garris, the Smiths, Charles and Chris, Darrin Robinson, Frenchy Tomlin and Harper Williams.

"No question he was in the same class as Matthews and Bagley," agrees Jim Kish, who coached both National Basketball Association players-to-be at Warren Harding—and who wouldn't allow Andrade to play at Harding because of his unwillingness to meet classroom standards.

"Ray was a guy with all the ability, on the same pedestal with [high school rival and future ABA/NBA star] John Williamson," George Thompson says. "He had a future that was painted in gold."

McLeod, who starred at Centenary University, and his cousin, Frank Oleynick, who was among the national scoring leaders for two seasons at

Seattle University and played for the NBA Seattle SuperSonics, idolized Andrade. They even patterned their game after his.

Luckett, whose fabulous early successes at Kolbe High School were tempered by a comparatively modest playing career at Ohio University and a failure to make the NBA Detroit Pistons, likened Andrade's style and mode of dress to Walt Frazier, the New York Knicks All-Star guard.

"[Andrade] was ahead of his time," Oleynick is quoted in *Chase the Game*, Pat Jordan's penetrating look at the basketball rivalry—and enduring bond—among Oleynick, McLeod and Luckett.

> *He invented the spin move in Bridgeport when he was only fifteen. He'd go dribbling up to your face and then peel off your hip, turning his back on you while carrying the ball on his hip. The first time he did that on Pitt Street we started yelling, "Sonny* ["Sonny James" was Andrade's pseudonym in the book], *you can't do that. That's carrying the ball!" He said, "You watch me." And sure enough, about then, who comes along but Clyde Frazier, and he gets away with it all the time. But Sonny was the first player I ever saw make the spin move.*

Andrade's 1969–70 season at Central, which at that juncture was the Bridgeport high school with the richest athletic tradition, placed him among the Park City's basketball elite. Although Rich Semo, a six-six forward who would receive All-American acclaim and a scholarship to Florida State, remains the name etched in most people's memories, Andrade was the Hilltoppers' catalyst, the playmaker who distributed crisp, often razzle-dazzle passes to Semo and other teammates. He also led the team in scoring with 22 points per game.

Penders, whose successes in the coaching ranks have garnered him a six-figure salary at Texas, was just twenty-four years old and in his first year as coach and business teacher at Central when Andrade arrived on the scene. Under Penders, the seventeen-year-old guard, who had been dismissed from Harding, flourished.

"[Penders] was one of the few people Ray would bend over backward for," remembers Kenny Sumpter, now the owner of a local limousine service. "Ray liked his approach to basketball, that whole [fast break] style of play. [Penders] wasn't big in being a disciplinarian. Because of that, they got to be friends. [Penders] went out of his way to keep Pudgy on the right track."

"He lived on the East Side, on Wilmot Avenue, and I used to pick him up for school every day," Penders recalled. "I wanted to be sure he got there. He went to school every day that year, and he did better than average work. He never gave me any trouble."

Reaching His Peak

Central averaged 99 points a game that winter. After an opening loss to Hillhouse of New Haven, the Hilltoppers reeled off twenty-three consecutive wins. Andrade, who had scored 39 points in a regular-season victory over Fairfield Prep, stepped up his game in the Class LL state tournament. Perhaps he was at his brilliant best in the Hilltoppers' opening-round 121–77 dismantling of Hartford Public, when he netted 32 points and directed the Central attack with aplomb.

"He was awesome on the attack," wrote Peter Putrimas in the *Bridgeport Post*, "bringing the ball up court by himself, dribbling around opponents at will, passing off fluidly to his teammates and scoring 22 points in the half."

Longtime observers of Connecticut high school basketball point to Central's semifinal battle with Wilbur Cross and championship meeting with Hillhouse that March as two of the most memorable games in tournament history. The Hilltoppers toppled Cross, 105–103, despite 39 points from John Williamson, before a capacity five thousand fans at Central Connecticut State University's Kaiser Gym. Andrade displayed his customary flamboyant floor leadership and contributed 16 points.

"He was absolutely incredible versus John Williamson," says Thompson.

McLeod, now a teacher at Blackham School in Bridgeport and assistant coach at Sacred Heart University, remembers that long-ago period for another reason. "New Haven basketball had the mystique. They always won," he related. "Pudgy always told me not to be intimidated by those New Haven guys. When they beat Cross that night, it turned everything around. He gave us the confidence to beat 'em."

Four days later, Central was rematched with Hillhouse for the state championship. The defending champion Academics held a 9-point lead in the final period, but the Hilltoppers, despite subpar shooting, fought back to tie, 78–78, in the closing fifteen seconds. The redoubtable

Andrade supplied the equalizer with a fifteen-foot jumper. Although the New Haven school would prevail on a last-second shot, Central had proven a point. Bridgeport schools did, indeed, belong on the same court.

He Couldn't Handle It

Ernest Parker, now the director of Bridgeport's Youth-at-Risk program, remembers: "It was a real culture shock to him, going from street hood and clever thief to being the best player in the city."

Away from basketball, Andrade did little to endear himself at Central, as had been the case during his unhappy stay at Harding. He put a modicum of effort into his studies—when he decided to show up for class. Opinions differ; some school sources contend he remained eligible during the basketball season, while others say his only passing grade was achieved in gym.

Ray's homeroom teacher, Andy Karcich, remembers him as "a thoroughly disagreeable young man when he was here. I took a real interest in him, I tried to help him, give him friendly advice, but he wouldn't listen. He was aloof," says Karcich, now the supervisor of Central's Magnet component.

Jim Roche, then Central's athletic director, said Andrade was "a tough kid, a problem. He'd come in for the basketball season and then leave school." Was he into drugs at that point? "As far as I knew, he was clean here," Roche responded.

Rhoada Kraus is retired now, after a lifetime of teaching English at Central and Bridgeport's other public high schools. She recalled Andrade as a student who "was never doing any of his classwork. As far as I remember, he couldn't read or write. He never had a paper or a pencil."

Parker, who had befriended a fourteen-year-old Andrade when he was "giving his mother and the rest of the family trouble," disputes a portion of Kraus's statement. "He had a phobia for school. He never got used to the classroom," he says.

But Parker claims Andrade's capacity for reading, even as a youngster, was more than adequate, and he possesses letters written by Ray at the federal penitentiary in Lewisburg, Pennsylvania. Much of Andrade's prose, he says, is well constructed and even lyrical.

Ernie Parker remained close to Andrade, providing guidance as a friend, coach, counselor and juvenile court probation officer. He made at least one visit to see him at the Eastern Correctional Institution in Napanoch, New York.

To hear Parker tell it, the minuses far outweighed the pluses in Andrade's life. "He had three, four early arrests for shoplifting, breaking into a school," Parker says. "He stole things from his mother and grandparents. After two, three more offenses, the judge committed him to the Connecticut School for Boys in Meriden."

His stay at Harding was a washout, and even the year at Central ended prematurely: Ray did not return to school after the state championship game. "He started getting a lot of favors from pimps in the neighborhood. He really played it to the hilt," recalls Parker. "And he was dabbling in heroin. He really started to look bad."

Penders, it was said, attempted to get Andrade back in school the following year, to rejoin the remainder of an otherwise-intact starting unit, but was overruled by the principal, Edward Tamashunas. The latter refused to comment on the matter.

However, it is Penders's recollection that Andrade had no intention of returning to Central following his "disappearance" that summer. "He came back from New York with a drug problem. He didn't want to come back to school," said the Texas coach.

Parker made one final attempt to keep Andrade in school and on a path to basketball stardom; he placed him in Laurinburg Institute, the North Carolina prep school whose alumni include the Providence College All-American Jimmy Walker. But it wasn't long before Parker received an upsetting phone call. "He's ruining my whole school," wailed the principal. "Get him out of here."

Arrested for armed robbery soon thereafter, Ray Andrade spent most of his remaining years in prison, in Lewisburg, Leavenworth, Kansas; Napanoch, New York; Somers, Connecticut; and other institutions. But apparently his basketball skills never eroded.

Last spring, McLeod was driving past Fairfield High School when he spotted a familiar figure on the basketball court. Barry parked his car, laced up his sneakers and joined the thirty-nine-year-old Andrade on the court. "He still had the aura, the flamboyance about him," McLeod recalls. "He was still passing the ball, he never missed a beat.

We played five-on-five for two and a half hours. I never had so much fun since I left college."

On January 14, 1992, McLeod and many others read the terrible front-page headline in the *Bridgeport Post*: "Store owner shoots, kills holdup man," accompanied by a four-color photograph of a Bridgeport police sergeant standing over the covered body. Poking out from under the shroud were Andrade's feet, covered with new sneakers.

According to police reports, Richard Nichio Sr., owner of the Crown Budget Market on Madison Avenue, saw the robbery in progress on the surveillance monitor in his office. Coming to the aid of his sixteen-year-old female cashier, Nichio confronted the gunman and, after Andrade pointed a gun at him, fired three shots. Andrade died at the scene. The state's attorney, citing the legal concept of the "defense of others," declined to indict Nichio for the shooting.

Ernie Parker sang "Come Yet Disconsolate" at Andrade's funeral. Barry McLeod, Frank Oleynick, Walter Luckett and others with whom he played basketball attended the wake. Kenny Sumpter was there, too.

"If he had the right direction, things could have been different," Sumpter said. But Ray Andrade's life had been out of control for a long time.

Fairfield County Advocate, February 27–March 4, 1992

Records

NUTMEGGERS IN NAISMITH MEMORIAL BASKETBALL HALL OF FAME

PLAYER (HOMETOWN)	TEAM	INDUCTED
Calvin Murphy (Norwalk)	Houston Rockets	1993

COACHES (HOMETOWN)	SCHOOLS	INDUCTED
Geno Auriemma	Connecticut	2006
Jim Calhoun	Northeastern, Connecticut	2005
Howard Cann (Bridgeport)	New York University	1968
Howard Hobson	Southern Oregon, Oregon, Yale	1965
Ken Loeffler	Geneva, Yale, LaSalle, Texas A&M	1964

CONTRIBUTORS (HOMETOWN)	CREDENTIALS	INDUCTED
J. Walter Kennedy (Stamford)	Commissioner, NBA	1981
Maurice Podoloff (New Haven)	Commissioner, NBA	1974
Elmer Ripley	Player, coach (Yale, 7 other schools)	1973
Amos Alonzo Stagg	Pioneer, coach (Yale)	1959

Nutmeggers in National Collegiate Basketball Hall of Fame

Player (hometown)	School	Inducted
Calvin Murphy (Norwalk)	Niagara	2006

Coaches (hometown)	Schools	Inducted
Jim Calhoun	Northeastern, Connecticut	2006
Howard Cann (Bridgeport)	New York University	2006
Howard Hobson	Southern Oregon, Oregon, Yale	2006
Ken Loeffler	Geneva, Yale, LaSalle, Texas A&M	2006

Contributor (hometown)	Credentials	Inducted
Joe Vancisin (Bridgeport)	Yale coach, administrator	2011

CONNECTICUT NATIVES IN NBA/ABA (33)

PLAYER	BIRTHPLACE	DOB	HT.	HIGH SCHOOL	COLLEGE	NBA/ABA CAREER (GAMES)
Michael Adams	Hartford	1-19-63	5-10	Hartford Public	Boston College	1985–96 (653)
Chuck Aleksinas	Litchfield	2-26-59	6-10	Wamogo	Kentucky; UConn	1984–85 (74)
Courtney Alexander	Bridgeport	4-27-77	6-5	Durham, NC	Virginia, Fresno St.	2000–3 (187)
John Bagley	Bridgeport	4-23-60	6-0	Warren Harding	Boston College	1982–94 (665)
Scott Burrell	New Haven	1-12-71	6-7	Hamden	Connecticut	1993–2001 (383)
Tom Callahan	Stamford	6-2-21	6-1	Stamford	Rockhurst	1946–47 (13)
* Marcus Camby	Hartford	3-22-74	6-11	Hartford Public	Massachusetts	1996– (890)
Keith Closs	Hartford	4-3-76	7-3	Baldwin Park, CA	Central Conn.	1997–2000 (130)
Chris Dudley	Stamford	2-22-65	6-11	Torrey Pines, CA	Yale	1987–03 (886)
Johnny Egan	Hartford	1-31-39	5-11	Weaver	Providence	1961–72 (712)
Billy Evans	New Haven	3-3-47	6-0	Hillhouse	Boston College	1969–70 (53)
John Garris	Bridgeport	6-6-59	6-8	Bassick	Michigan, Boston College	1983–84 (33)
Mike Gminski	Monroe	8-3-59	6-11	Masuk	Duke	1980–94 (938)
Ryan Gomes	Waterbury	9-1-82	6-7	Wilby	Providence	2005– (450)

PLAYER	BIRTHPLACE	DOB	HT.	HIGH SCHOOL	COLLEGE	NBA/ABA CAREER (GAMES)
Jim Johnstone	New Canaan	9-20-60	6-11	Youngstown, NY	Wake Forest	1982–83 (23)
Bobby Knight	Hartford	1931	6-2	Weaver	none	1954–55 (2)
Bruce Kuczenski	Bristol	2-3-61	6-10	Bristol Central	Connecticut	1983–84 (15)
Rick Mahorn	Hartford	9-21-58	6-10	Weaver	Hampton Institute	1980–99 (1117)
Tharon Mayes	New Haven	9-9-68	6-3	Hillhouse	Florida State	1991–92 (24)
*Calvin Murphy	Norwalk	5-9-48	5-9	Norwalk	Niagara	1970–83 (1002)
Jay Murphy	Meriden	6-26-62	6-9	Maloney	Boston College	1984–88 (67)
Bob Nash	Hartford	8-24-50	6-8	Hartford Public	Hawaii	1972–75, ’77–79 (236)
Frank Oleynick	Bridgeport	2-20-55	6-2	Notre Dame Ffld.	Seattle	1975–77 (102)
Worthy Patterson	New Haven	6-17-31	6-2	Greenwich	Connecticut	1957–58 (4)
John Pinone	Hartford	2-19-61	6-8	South Catholic	Villanova	1983–84 (7)
Charles Smith	Bridgeport	7-16-65	6-10	Warren Harding	Pittsburgh	1988–97 (564)
Chris Smith	Bridgeport	5-17-70	6-3	Kolbe Cathedral	Connecticut	1992–95 (224)
Will Solomon	Hartford	7-20-78	6-1	East Hartford	Clemson	2001–2, ’08–9 (115)
Greg Stokes	New Haven	8-5-63	6-10	Hamilton, OH	Iowa	1985–86, ’89–90 (42)
Corny Thompson	Middletown	2-5-60	6-8	Middletown	Connecticut	1982–83 (44)

Player	Birthplace	DOB	Ht.	High School	College	NBA/ABA Career (Games)
Tyson Wheeler	New Britain	10-8-75	5-10	New London	Rhode Island	1998-99 (1)
Sly Williams	New Haven	1-26-58	6-7	Lee	Rhode Island	1979-86 (305)
John Williamson	New Haven	11-10-51	6-2	Wilbur Cross	New Mexico St.	1973-81 (516)

Bold indicates active through 2010-11 season

* Member of Naismith Memorial Basketball Hall of Fame

OTHERS WITH CONNECTICUT HIGH SCHOOL TIES IN NBA (13)

Player	Birthplace	DOB	Ht.	High School	College	NBA/ABA Career (Games)
Vin Baker	Lake Wales, FL	11-23-71	6-11	Old Saybrook	Hartford	1993-2006 (791)
Andray Blatche	**Syracuse, NY**	**8-22-86**	**6-11**	**South Kent Prep**	**none**	**2005– (383)**
Yinka Dare	Kano, Nigeria	10-10-72	7-0	Milford Academy	George Washington	1995-98 (110)
Vinny Del Negro	Springfield, MA	8-9-66	6-4	Suffield Academy	N. Carolina St.	1988-90, '92-2002 (771)
Quincy Douby	Brooklyn, NY	5-16-84	6-3	St. Thomas More	Rutgers	2006-9 (143)
Devin Ebanks	**Queens, NY**	**10-28-89**	**6-9**	**St. Thomas More**	**West Virginia**	**2010– (20)**
Rod Foster	Birmingham, AL	10-10-60	6-1	St. Thomas Aquinas	UCLA	1983-86 (207)
Deng Gai	Sudan	3-22-82	6-9	Milford Academy	Fairfield	2005-6 (2)
Wes Matthews	Sarasota, FL	8-24-59	6-1	Warren Harding	Wisconsin	1980-90 (465)

PLAYER	BIRTHPLACE	DOB	HT.	HIGH SCHOOL	COLLEGE	NBA/ABA CAREER (GAMES)
Paul McCracken	New York	9-11-50	6-4	Hillhouse	Cal St.–Northridge	1972–74, '76–77 (37)
Jerome Moiso	Paris, France	6-15-78	6-10	Milford Academy	UCLA	2000–5 (145)
Harold Pressley	Bronx, NY	7-14-63	6-7	St. Bernard	Villanova	1986–90 (299)
Dorell Wright	**Los Angeles**	**12-2-85**	**6-7**	**South Kent Prep**	**none**	**2004– (293)**

Bold indicates active through 2010–11 season

CONNECTICUT NATIVES WHO COACHED IN NBA/ABA (5)

PLAYER	BIRTHPLACE	DOB	HIGH SCHOOL	COLLEGE	TEAM, CAREER	W-L
John Castellani	New Britain	8-23-26	New Britain	Notre Dame	Minneapolis, 1959–60	11-25
Vince Cazzetta	New Britain	9-24-25	New Britain	Arnold	Pittsburgh ABA, 1967–68	54-24
Johnny Egan	Hartford	1-31-39	Weaver	Providence	Houston, 1972–76	129-152
Bob Staak	Darien	12-22-47	Darien	Connecticut	Washington, 1997	0-1
Tom Thibodeau	**New Britain**	**1-17-58**	**New Britain**	**Salem State**	**Chicago, 2010–**	**62-20**

Bold indicates active through 2010–11 season

Connecticut High School Alumni in NBA/ABA

Bassick, Bridgeport (1)—John Garris
Bristol Central (1)—Bruce Kuczenski
East Hartford (1)—Will Solomon
Greenwich (1)—Worthy Patterson
Hamden (1)—Scott Burrell
Hartford Public (3)—Michael Adams, Marcus Camby, Bob Nash
Hillhouse, New Haven (3)—Billy Evans, Tharon Mayes, Paul McCracken
Kolbe Cathedral, Bridgeport (1)—Chris Smith
Lee, New Haven (1)—Sly Williams
Maloney, Meriden (1)—Jay Murphy
Masuk, Monroe (1)—Mike Gminski
Middletown (1)—Corny Thompson
Milford Academy (3)—Yinka Dare, Deng Gai, Jerome Moiso
New London (1)—Tyson Wheeler
Norwalk (1)—Calvin Murphy
Notre Dame, Fairfield (1)—Frank Oleynick
Old Saybrook (1)—Vin Baker
St. Bernard, Uncasville (1)—Harold Pressley
St. Thomas Aquinas, New Britain (1)—Rod Foster
St. Thomas More, Oakdale (2)—Quincy Douby, Devin Ebanks
South Catholic, Hartford (1)—John Pinone
South Kent Prep (2)—Andray Blatche, Dorell Wright
Stamford (1)—Tom Callahan
Suffield Academy (1)—Vinny Del Negro
Wamogo, Litchfield (1)—Chuck Aleksinas
Warren Harding, Bridgeport (3)—John Bagley, Wes Matthews, Charles Smith
Weaver, Hartford (3)—Johnny Egan, Bobby Knight, Rick Mahorn
Wilbur Cross, New Haven (1)—John Williamson
Wilby, Waterbury (1)—Ryan Gomes

Connecticut College Alumni in NBA/ABA

(Connecticut hometown in parentheses when applicable)
Central Connecticut State University (2)—Keith Closs (Hartford), Corsley Edwards
Fairfield University (2)—Deng Gai, A.J. Wynder
University of Bridgeport (1)—Manute Bol
University of Connecticut (31)—Jeff Adrien, Chuck Aleksinas (Litchfield), Ray Allen, Hilton Armstrong, Wes Bialosuknia, Josh Boone, Scott Burrell (Hamden), Caron Butler, Khalid El-Amin, Jimmy Foster, Rudy Gay, Tate George, Ben Gordon, Richard Hamilton, Toby Kimball, Travis Knight, Bruce Kuczenski (Bristol), Donny Marshall, Donyell Marshall, Emeka Okafor, Kevin Ollie, Worthy Patterson (New Haven), A.J. Price, Clifford Robinson, Chris Smith (Bridgeport), Hasheem Thabeet, Corny Thompson (Middletown), Charlie Villanueva, Jake Voskuhl, Kemba Walker, Marcus Williams
University of Hartford (1)—Vin Baker (Old Saybrook)
Yale University (3)—Chris Dudley (Stamford), Earl "Butch" Graves Jr., Tony Lavelli Jr.

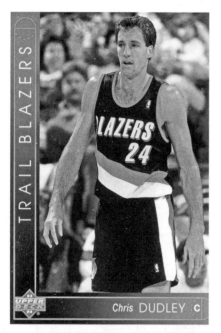

NBA players with a Connecticut imprint. *Clockwise from left*: Chris Dudley (Stamford native, Yale star), 1994 Upper Deck; Manute Bol (University of Bridgeport All-American), 1994 Upper Deck; Rick Mahorn (Hartford Public), 1982 Topps; Mike Gminski (Masuk of Monroe All-Stater), 1994 Upper Deck; *Courtesy of Frank Corr.*

Records

Outstanding NBA/ABA Performances

Defensive Player of the Year

Player (hometown/school)	Team	Season
Marcus Camby (Hartford)	Denver	2006–7

Sixth Man of the Year

Player (hometown/school)	Team	Season
Clifford Robinson (UConn)	Portland	1992–93
Ben Gordon (UConn)	Chicago	2004–5

Rookie of the Year

Player (hometown/school)	Team	Season
Emeka Okafor (UConn)	Charlotte	2004–5

Coach of the Year

Player (hometown)	Team	Season
Vince Cazzetta (New Britain)	Pittsburgh ABA	1967–68
Tom Thibodeau (New Britain)	Chicago	2010–11

J. Walter Kennedy Citizenship Award

Player (hometown/school)	Team	Season
Calvin Murphy (Norwalk)	Houston	1978–79
Chris Dudley (Stamford/Yale)	Portland	1995–96

All-NBA Team

Player (hometown/school)	Team	Season
Vin Baker (Old Saybrook/U. Hartford)	Milwaukee	1996–97 (third team), 1997–98 (second team)
Ray Allen (UConn)	Milwaukee	2000–1 (third team), 2004–5 (second team)

165

All-Defensive Team

PLAYER (HOMETOWN/SCHOOL)	TEAM	SEASON
Manute Bol (U. Bridgeport)	Washington	1985–86 (second team)
Rick Mahorn (Hartford)	Philadelphia	1989–90 (second team)
Clifford Robinson (UConn)	Phoenix, Detroit	1999–2000 (second team), 2001–2 (second team)
Marcus Camby (Hartford)	Denver	2004–5 (second team), 2005–6 (second team), 2006–7, 2007–8

All-Rookie Team

PLAYER (HOMETOWN/SCHOOL)	TEAM	SEASON
Calvin Murphy (Norwalk)	San Diego	1970–71
John Williamson (New Haven)	New York ABA	1973–74
Charles Smith (Bridgeport)	L.A. Clippers	1988–89
Vin Baker (Old Saybrook/U. Hartford)	Milwaukee	1993–94
Donyell Marshall (UConn)	Minn.-Golden State	1994–95 (second team)
Marcus Camby (Hartford)	Denver	1996–97
Ray Allen (UConn)	Milwaukee	1996–97 (second team)
Travis Knight (UConn)	L.A. Lakers	1996–97 (second team)
Courtney Alexander (Bridgeport)	Dallas-Wash.	2000–1 (second team)
Caron Butler (UConn)	Miami	2002–3
Ben Gordon (UConn)	Chicago	2004–5
Emeka Okafor (UConn)	Charlotte	2004–5
Charlie Villanueva (UConn)	Toronto	2005–6
Ryan Gomes (Waterbury)	Boston	2005–6 (second team)
Rudy Gay (UConn)	Memphis	2006–7
Marcus Williams (UConn)	New Jersey	2006–7 (second team)

Records

Championship Finals Participants

PLAYER (HOMETOWN/SCHOOL)	TEAM	YEARS	RESULT
Johnny Egan (Hartford)	L.A. Lakers	1969	Lost to Boston, 4-3
		1970	Lost to N.Y. Knicks, 4-3
John Williamson (New Haven)	New York ABA	1974	Def. Utah, 4-1
		1976	Def. Denver, 4-2
Calvin Murphy (Norwalk)	Houston	1981	Lost to Boston, 4-2
Wes Matthews (Bridgeport)	L.A. Lakers	1987	Def. Boston, 4-2
		1988	Def. Detroit, 4-3
Rick Mahorn (Hartford)	Detroit	1989	Def. Los Angeles, 4-0
Clifford Robinson (UConn)	Portland	1990	Lost to Detroit, 4-1
		1992	Lost to Chicago, 4-2
Charles Smith (Bridgeport)	New York	1994	Lost to Houston, 4-3
Scott Burrell (Hamden/UConn)	Chicago	1998	Def. Utah, 4-2
Marcus Camby (Hartford)	New York	1999	Lost to San Antonio, 4-1
Chris Dudley (Stamford/Yale)	New York	1999	Lost to San Antonio, 4-1
Travis Knight (UConn)	L.A. Lakers	2000	Def. Indiana, 4-2
Kevin Ollie (UConn)	Philadelphia	2001	Lost to Los Angeles, 4-1
Richard Hamilton (UConn)	Detroit	2004	Def. Los Angeles, 4-1
		2005	Lost to San Antonio, 4-3
Donyell Marshall (UConn)	Cleveland	2007	Lost to San Antonio, 4-0
Ray Allen (UConn)	Boston	2008	Def. Los Angeles, 4-2
		2010	Lost to Los Angeles, 4-3

All-Star Game Participants

PLAYER (HOMETOWN/SCHOOL)	TEAM	YEARS	HIGHLIGHT
Jimmy Foster (UConn)	Denver ABA	1974	scoreless
Calvin Murphy (Norwalk)	Houston	1979	3-5 FG, 6 pts., 5 assts.
Michael Adams (Hartford)	Washington	1992	4-8 FG, 9 pts.
Clifford Robinson (UConn)	Portland	1994	5-8 FG, 10 pts.
Vin Baker (Old Saybrook/U. Hartford)	Milwaukee, Seattle	1995, '96, '97, '98	19 pts., 12 rebs., 1997
Ray Allen (UConn)	Milwaukee, Seattle, Boston	2000, '01, '02, '04, '05, '06, '07, '08, '09, '11	28 pts., 2008
Richard Hamilton (UConn)	Detroit	2006, '07, '08	9 pts., 2008
Caron Butler (UConn)	Washington	2007	4 rebs.

Although Michael Adams stood just five-ten, the 1981 Hartford Public High All-Stater became a star at Boston College (All–Big East, 1,650 career points) and during an eleven-season career in the NBA. A prolific 3-point shooter, he averaged 26.5 points per game with the Denver Nuggets in 1990–91, placing sixth in the league, and also ranked third with 10.5 assists per game. *Courtesy of Denver Nuggets.*

Records

Points Per Game

PLAYER (HOMETOWN/SCHOOL)	TEAM	PPG (RANK)	SEASON
Calvin Murphy (Norwalk)	Houston	25.6 (5th)	1977–78

Rebounds Per Game

PLAYER (HOMETOWN/SCHOOL)	TEAM	RPG (RANK)	SEASON
Emeka Okafor (UConn)	Charlotte	10.9 (4th)	2004–5
Marcus Camby (Hartford)	Denver	11.7 (5th)	2006–7
Marcus Camby (Hartford)	Denver	13.1 (2nd)	2007–8
Emeka Okafor (UConn)	Charlotte	10.1 (5th)	2008–9
Marcus Camby (Hartford)	L.A. Clip/Port.	11.8 (2nd)	2009–10

Assists Per Game

PLAYER (HOMETOWN/SCHOOL)	TEAM	APG (RANK)	SEASON
Johnny Egan (Hartford)	Det./N.Y. Knicks	5.4 (5th)	1963–64
Calvin Murphy (Norwalk)	Houston	7.4 (2nd)	1973–74
Calvin Murphy (Norwalk)	Houston	7.3 (3rd)	1975–76
John Bagley (Bridgeport)	Cleveland	8.6 (5th)	1984–85
John Bagley (Bridgeport)	Cleveland	9.4 (4th)	1985–86
Michael Adams (Hartford)	Denver	10.5 (3rd)	1990–91

Field Goal Percentage

PLAYER (HOMETOWN/SCHOOL)	TEAM	PCT. (RANK)	SEASON
Calvin Murphy (Norwalk)	Houston	.522 (4th)	1973–74
Vin Baker (Old Saybrook/ Hartford)	Seattle	.542 (5th)	1997–98
Marcus Camby (Hartford)	N.Y. Knicks	.524 (3rd)	2000–1
Donyell Marshall (UConn)	Utah	.519 (3rd)	2001–2
Emeka Okafor (UConn)	New Orleans	.573 (3rd)	2010–11

3-Point Field-Goal Percentage

PLAYER (HOMETOWN/SCHOOL)	TEAM	PCT. (RANK)	SEASON
Wes Bialosuknia (UConn)	Oakland ABA	.397 (2nd)	1967–68
Richard Hamilton (UConn)	Detroit	.458 (1st)	2005–6
Ray Allen (UConn)	Boston	.444 (2nd)	2010–11

Free Throw Percentage

PLAYER (HOMETOWN/SCHOOL)	TEAM	PCT. (RANK)	SEASON
Calvin Murphy (Norwalk)	Houston	.890 (2nd)	1971–72
Calvin Murphy (Norwalk)	Houston	.888 (2nd)	1972–73
Calvin Murphy (Norwalk)	Houston	.883 (2nd)	1974–75
Calvin Murphy (Norwalk)	Houston	.907 (2nd)	1975–76
Calvin Murphy (Norwalk)	Houston	.886 (3rd)	1976–77
Calvin Murphy (Norwalk)	Houston	.918 (2nd)	1977–78
Calvin Murphy (Norwalk)	Houston	.928 (2nd)	1978–79
Calvin Murphy (Norwalk)	Houston	.897 (2nd)	1979–80
Calvin Murphy (Norwalk)	Houston	.958 (1st)	1980–81
Calvin Murphy (Norwalk)	Houston	.920 (1st)	1982–83
Mike Gminski (Monroe)	New Jersey	.893 (3rd)	1985–86
Mike Gminski (Monroe)	N.J./Phila.	.906 (4th)	1987–88
Ray Allen (UConn)	Milwaukee	.875 (3rd)	1997–98
Ray Allen (UConn)	Milwaukee	.903 (4th)	1998–99
Ray Allen (UConn)	Milwaukee	.887 (5th)	1999–2000
Richard Hamilton (UConn)	Washington	.890 (2nd)	2001–2
Ray Allen (UConn)	Milwaukee/Seattle	.916 (2nd)	2002–3
Ray Allen (UConn)	Seattle	.904 (4th)	2003–4
Ray Allen (UConn)	Seattle	.902 (3rd)	2005–6
Ray Allen (UConn)	Seattle	.903 (4th)	2006–7

Records

Player (hometown/school)	Team	Pct. (rank)	Season
Ray Allen (UConn)	Boston	.907 (4th)	2007–8
Ben Gordon (UConn)	Chicago	.908 (3rd)	2007–8
Ray Allen (UConn)	Boston	.952 (2nd)	2008–9
Ray Allen (UConn)	Boston	.913 (3rd)	2009–10

Blocks Per Game

Player (hometown/school)	Team	BPG (rank)	Season
Manute Bol (U. Bridgeport)	Washington	5.0 (1st)	1985–86
Manute Bol (U. Bridgeport)	Washington	3.7 (2nd)	1986–87
Manute Bol (U. Bridgeport)	Washington	2.7 (5th)	1987–88
Manute Bol (U. Bridgeport)	Golden State	4.3 (1st)	1988–89
Manute Bol (U. Bridgeport)	Golden State	3.2 (4th)	1989–90
Manute Bol (U. Bridgeport)	Philadelphia	3.0 (4th)	1990–91
Chris Dudley (Stamford/Yale)	New Jersey	2.5 (5th)	1990–91
Marcus Camby (Hartford)	Toronto	3.7 (1st)	1997–98
Marcus Camby (Hartford)	Denver	2.6 (5th)	2003–4
Marcus Camby (Hartford)	Denver	3.0 (2nd)	2004–5
Marcus Camby (Hartford)	Denver	3.3 (1st)	2005–6
Marcus Camby (Hartford)	Denver	3.3 (1st)	2006–7
Emeka Okafor (UConn)	Charlotte	2.6 (4th)	2006–7
Marcus Camby (Hartford)	Denver	3.6 (1st)	2007–8
Marcus Camby (Hartford)	L.A. Clippers	2.1 (3rd)	2008–9
Marcus Camby (Hartford)	L.A. Clip./Port.	2.0 (5th)	2009–10

Steals Per Game

Player (hometown/school)	Team	SPG (rank)	Season
Caron Butler (UConn)	Washington	2.1 (3rd)	2006–7
Caron Butler (UConn)	Washington	2.2 (4th)	2007–8

OUTSTANDING COLLEGIATE PERFORMANCES

Player of the Year

PLAYER (HOMETOWN)	SCHOOL	SEASON	SELECTOR
Gilmore Kinney	Yale	1906–7	Helms Foundation
Howard Cann (Bridgeport)	New York U.	1919–20	Helms Foundation
Tony Lavelli Jr.	Yale	1948–49	Helms Foundation
Marcus Camby (Hartford)	Massachusetts	1995–96	Naismith, NABC, AP
Emeka Okafor	Connecticut	2003–4	shared NABC Award with Jameer Nelson, St. Joseph's

Yale All-American Tony Lavelli, a six-three forward with an accurate long-range hook shot, led the nation's collegians in scoring with a 22.4 average in 1948–49. Drafted by the Boston Celtics, he averaged 8.8 points per game in his rookie pro season but became best known for playing his accordion during halftime at Boston Garden and at certain other arenas. After retiring from basketball, he embarked on a long career as a nightclub performer and songwriter. *Courtesy of Yale University Sports Information.*

Records

Coach of the Year

COACH (HOMETOWN)	SCHOOL	SEASON	SELECTOR
Jim Calhoun	Connecticut	1989–90	AP, UPI, Sporting News, CBS/Chevrolet

Defensive Player of the Year

PLAYER (HOMETOWN)	SCHOOL	SEASON
Emeka Okafor	Connecticut	2002–3, 2003–4
Hasheem Thabeet	Connecticut	2007–8, 2008–9

Final Four Most Outstanding Player

PLAYER (HOMETOWN)	SCHOOL	SEASON
Richard Hamilton	Connecticut	1998–99
Emeka Okafor	Connecticut	2003–4
Kemba Walker	Connecticut	2010–11

CONSENSUS ALL-AMERICANS FROM CONNECTICUT

PLAYER (HOMETOWN)	SCHOOL	SEASON
Gus Broberg (Torrington)	Dartmouth	1939–40, 1940–41
Tony Lavelli Jr.	Yale	1945–46 (second team), 1947–48 (second team), 1948–49
Calvin Murphy (Norwalk)	Niagara	1967–68 (second team), 1968–69, 1969–70
Mike Gminski (Monroe)	Duke	1978–79, 1979–80 (second team)
Sly Williams (New Haven)	Rhode Island	1978–79 (second team)
Donyell Marshall	Connecticut	1993–94
Ray Allen	Connecticut	1995–96
Marcus Camby (Hartford)	Massachusetts	1995–96
Richard Hamilton	Connecticut	1997–98 (second team), 1998–99

Gustave "Gus" Broberg, from Torrington, was a two-time consensus All-American at Dartmouth, 1939–40 and 1940–41. A U.S. Marine pilot during World War II, he lost his right arm when his plane crashed in Okinawa. The resilient Broberg taught himself to write with his left hand, earned a law degree from the University of Virginia and practiced law and served as a judge in Palm Beach, Florida. His son, Pete Broberg, pitched in baseball's Major Leagues for seven seasons. *Courtesy of Dartmouth College Sports Information.*

Ryan Gomes, from Wilby High of Waterbury, developed into a consensus All-American at Providence College and was chosen by the Boston Celtics on the second round of the 2005 NBA draft. He's been a solid pro for six seasons. *Courtesy of Providence College Media Relations.*

PLAYER (HOMETOWN)	SCHOOL	SEASON
Courtney Alexander (Bridgeport)	Fresno State	1999–2000 (second team)
Emeka Okafor	Connecticut	2003–4
Ryan Gomes (Waterbury)	Providence	2004–5
Rudy Gay	Connecticut	2005–6 (second team)
Hasheem Thabeet	Connecticut	2008–9 (second team)
Kemba Walker	Connecticut	2010–11

OTHER ALL-AMERICAN SELECTIONS FROM CONNECTICUT

National Association of Basketball Coaches

PLAYER (HOMETOWN)	SCHOOL	SEASON
Art Quimby (New London)	Connecticut	1954–55 (second team)
Tony Hanson (Waterbury)	Connecticut	1976–77 (fifth team)
John Bagley (Bridgeport)	Boston College	1981–82 (third team)
Charles Smith (Bridgeport)	Pittsburgh	1987–88 (second team)
Ray Allen	Connecticut	1994–95 (third team)
Emeka Okafor	Connecticut	2002–3 (third team)

U.S. Basketball Writers Association

PLAYER (HOMETOWN)	SCHOOL	SEASON
A.J. Price	Connecticut	2007–8 (second team)

Associated Press

PLAYER (HOMETOWN)	SCHOOL	SEASON
John Pinone (Hartford)	Villanova	1982–83 (third team)

United Press International

PLAYER (HOMETOWN)	SCHOOL	SEASON
Doron Sheffer	Connecticut	1995–96 (third team)

APPENDIX

Converse

Player (Hometown)	School	Season
Tony Lavelli Jr.	Yale	1946–47 (third team)

Helms Athletic Foundation

Player (Hometown)	School	Season
Harry Fisher	Yale	1904–5
Willard Hyatt	Yale	1904–5
Gilmore Kinney	Yale	1904–5, 1906–7
Julian Hayward	Wesleyan	1907–8, 1908–9
Haskell Noyes	Yale	1907–8
Edward Hayward	Wesleyan	1912–13
W.P. Arnold	Yale	1914–15
Ollie Kinney	Yale	1916–17
Charles Taft	Yale	1916–17
Howard Cann (Bridgeport)	New York U.	1919–20
Gus Broberg (Torrington)	Dartmouth	1938–39
Rick Kaminsky	Yale	1963–64

ACADEMIC ALL-AMERICANS

Player (Hometown)	School	Season
Wes Bialosuknia	Connecticut	1966–67
Ken Bicknell	U.S. Coast Guard Academy	1970–71
James Akin (West Hartford)	Wesleyan	1971–72
Rich Fairbrother (West Hartford)	Wesleyan	1973–74
Mike Gminski (Monroe)	Duke	1977–78, 1978–79, 1979–80
John Pinone (Hartford)	Villanova	1981–82, 1982–83

Player (hometown)	School	Season
Steve Maizes	Wesleyan	1981–82
Harold Jensen (Trumbull)	Villanova	1985–86, 1986–87
Keith Wolff (Ellington)	Trinity	1995–96
Emeka Okafor	Connecticut	2002–3, 2003–4
Tim Abromaitis (Unionville)	Notre Dame	2009–10, 2010–11

NCAA Division II All-Americans
National Association of Basketball Coaches

Player (hometown)	School	Season
Gary Baum	Bridgeport	1968–69
Howie Dickenman (Norwich)	Central Conn. State	1968–69
Bill Reaves (New Haven)	Central Conn. State	1969–70 (second team), 1970–71 (second team)
Ed Czernota (Bridgeport)	Sacred Heart	1971–72
Ray Vyzas	Sacred Heart	1972–73 (second team)
Peter Egan (West Hartford)	Hartford	1973–74 (second team), 1974–75 (second team)
Lee Hollerbach	Bridgeport	1975–76
Harold Driver	Quinnipiac	1975–76 (second team), 1977–78 (third team)
Andre Means	Sacred Heart	1976–77 (second team), 1977–78
Frank Gugliotta	Bridgeport	1976–77 (third team)
Carl Winfree	Sacred Heart	1976–77 (third team)
Hector Olivencia	Sacred Heart	1977–78
Mark Noon (Bristol)	Hartford	1977–78 (third team), 1978–79
Rick Mahorn (Hartford)	Hampton	1978–79 (second team), 1979-80 (second team)
Jerry Steuerer	Bridgeport	1978–79 (third team)
Keith Bennett (Stamford)	Sacred Heart	1980–81 (second team), 1981–82, 1982–83

PLAYER (HOMETOWN)	SCHOOL	SEASON
Steve Ayers (Wethersfield)	Central Conn. State	1980–81 (third team), 1981–82 (second team)
Tony Gonzalez (New Britain)	Southern Conn. St.	1981–82 (third team)
Rich Leonard (New Britain)	Central Conn. State	1982–83 (second team), 1983–84 (second team)
Rhonie Wright	Sacred Heart	1982–83 (third team)
Manute Bol	Bridgeport	1984–85
Roger Younger (Middletown)	Sacred Heart	1984–85 (second team), 1985–86
Bill Bayno	Sacred Heart	1984–85 (third team)
Norman Taylor	Bridgeport	1986–87 (third team)
Herb Watkins	New Haven	1987–88
Tony Judkins (Hartford)	Sacred Heart	1987–88 (third team), 1988–89 (second team)
Lambert Shell	Bridgeport	1989–90 (second team), 1990–91, 1991–92
Gary Battle	University of New Haven	1989–90 (third team)
Darrin Robinson (Bridgeport)	Sacred Heart	1991–92 (second team), 1992–93
Alex Wright (Bridgeport)	Central Oklahoma	1992–93 (Player of the Year)
Lamont Jones	Bridgeport	1992–93 (second team), 1994–95
Rob Paternostro (Waterbury)	New Hampshire Col.	1994–95 (second team)
T.J. Trimboli (Norwalk)	Southern Conn. State	1999–2000 (second team)
Tom Baudinet (Watertown)	St. Anselm	2010–11

NCAA DIVISION II COACH OF THE YEAR
National Association of Basketball Coaches

COACH (HOMETOWN)	SCHOOL	SEASON
Dave Bike (Bridgeport)	Sacred Heart	1985–86
Bruce Webster	Bridgeport	1991–92

NCAA DIVISION III ALL-AMERICANS

PLAYER (HOMETOWN)	SCHOOL	SEASON
Tod Hart (Waterbury)	Ithaca	1981–82 (second team), 1982–83 (third team)
Ken Abere	Trinity	1984–85 (third team)
Zack Smith	Connecticut College	1998–99 (second team)
Kareem Tatum	Connecticut College	1999–2000 (second team)
Colin Tabb (Somers)	Trinity	2001–2
Brice Assic	Western Conn. State	2004–5 (second team)
Tyler Rhoten	Trinity	2005–6

NAIA ALL-AMERICANS

PLAYER (HOMETOWN)	SCHOOL	SEASON
Alvin Clinkscales (Bridgeport)	Bridgeport	1953–54 (third team)
Don Perrelli (New Haven)	Southern Conn. St.	1959–60 (second team)
Gary Liberatore (New Canaan)	New Haven	1965–66
Ron Riordan	New Haven	1968–69 (third team), 1969–70 (third team), 1970–71 (third team)
Rasuel McKune	Teikyo Post	1995–96 (second team)

Gary Liberatore, of New Canaan, amassed 3,176 points—a record for New England collegians—during his four-year career at then–New Haven College. He was voted an NAIA All-American in 1965–66. *Courtesy of University of New Haven Athletic Communications.*

CONNECTICUT PLAYERS IN THE OLYMPICS

PLAYER (HOMETOWN / SCHOOL)	NBA TEAM	YEAR	SITE
Charles Smith (Bridgeport/ Pittsburgh)	L.A. Clippers	1988	Seoul, South Korea
Ray Allen (Connecticut)	Milwaukee	2000	Sydney, Australia
Vin Baker (Old Saybrook/U. Hartford)	Seattle	2000	Sydney, Australia
Emeka Okafor (Connecticut)	Charlotte	2004	Athens, Greece

CONNECTICUT COLLEGIANS AMONG NATIONAL LEADERS

Points Per Game

PLAYER (HOMETOWN)	SCHOOL	PPG (RANK)	SEASON
Walt Dropo (Moosup)	Connecticut	21.7 (9th)	1942–43
Tony Lavelli Jr.	Yale	21.3 (8th)	1945–46
Tony Lavelli Jr.	Yale	20.5 (3rd)	1947–48
Tony Lavelli Jr.	Yale	22.4 (1st)	1948–49
Wes Bialosuknia	Connecticut	28.0 (5th)	1966–67
Calvin Murphy (Norwalk)	Niagara	38.2 (2nd)	1967–68
Calvin Murphy (Norwalk)	Niagara	32.4 (3rd)	1968–69
Calvin Murphy (Norwalk)	Niagara	29.4 (8th)	1969–70
John Williamson (New Haven)	New Mexico St.	27.1 (6th)	1971–72
John Williamson (New Haven)	New Mexico St.	27.2 (9th)	1972–73
Frank Oleynick (Bridgeport)	Seattle	25.1 (7th)	1973–74
Frank Oleynick (Bridgeport)	Seattle	27.3 (7th)	1974–75
Tony Hanson (Waterbury)	Connecticut	26.0 (10th)	1976–77
Vin Baker (Old Saybrook)	Hartford	27.6 (2nd)	1991–92
Vin Baker (Old Saybrook)	Hartford	28.3 (4th)	1992–93
Doremus Bennerman (Bridgeport)	Siena	26.0 (7th)	1993–94

Records

Left: Frank Oleynick, from Bridgeport, ranked seventh among the nation's scorers for two straight years at Seattle University. He also topped the country in 1974–75 with a .888 free throw percentage. He played two seasons with the NBA Seattle SuperSonics. *Courtesy of Seattle University Sports Information.*

Below, left: Wes Bialosuknia, one of the outstanding long-range shooters in UConn basketball history, fires up a jumper versus Rutgers. He averaged 28 points per game as a senior in 1966–67, ranking fifth nationally. *Courtesy of University of Connecticut Athletic Communications.*

Below, right: Toby Kimball, who led the nation in rebounding as a senior with 21.0 per game in 1964–65, registers two points for UConn. *Courtesy of University of Connecticut Athletic Communications.*

PLAYER (HOMETOWN)	SCHOOL	PPG (RANK)	SEASON
Ray Allen	Connecticut	23.4 (10th)	1995–96
Courtney Alexander (Bridgeport)	Fresno St.	24.8 (1st)	1999–2000
Rob Monroe	Quinnipiac	22.7 (5th)	2004–5
Quincy Douby	Rutgers	25.4 (6th)	2005–6
Robert McKiver (New Haven)	Houston	23.6 (8th)	2007–8
Kemba Walker	Connecticut	23.5 (5th)	2010–11

Rebounds Per Game

PLAYER (HOMETOWN)	SCHOOL	RPG (RANK)	SEASON
Art Quimby (New London)	Connecticut	20.5 (4th)	1952–53
Art Quimby (New London)	Connecticut	22.6 (1st)	1953–54
Art Quimby (New London)	Connecticut	24.4 (2nd)	1954–55
Toby Kimball	Connecticut	17.3 (8th)	1963–64
Toby Kimball	Connecticut	21.0 (1st)	1964–65
Mike Branch (New Haven)	Fairfield	16.0 (8th)	1964–65
Mike Branch (New Haven)	Fairfield	16.6 (7th)	1965–66
Mark Frazer	Fairfield	15.7 (10th)	1970–71
John Thomas	Connecticut	13.9 (5th)	1975–76
Chris Dudley (Stamford)	Yale	13.3 (2nd)	1986–87
Gerry Besselink	Connecticut	10.7 (9th)	1986–87
Tyrone Canino (Hartford)	Central Conn. State	11.5 (6th)	1987–88
Drew Henderson	Fairfield	11.4 (10th)	1991–92
Darren Phillip	Fairfield	14.0 (1st)	1999–2000
Jeremy Bishop	Quinnipiac	12.0 (1st)	2001–2
Emeka Okafor	Connecticut	11.2 (7th)	2002–3
Emeka Okafor	Connecticut	11.5 (3rd)	2003–4
Kenny Adeleke	Hartford	13.1 (2nd)	2005–6

Records

Player (hometown)	School	RPG (rank)	Season
Obie Nwadike	Central Conn. State	10.7 (6th)	2006–07
Damian Saunders (Waterbury)	Duquesne	11.3 (6th)	2009–10
Justin Rutty	Quinnipiac	10.9 (8th)	2009–10
Jordan Williams (Torrington)	Maryland	11.8 (3rd)	2010–11

Assists Per Game

Player (hometown)	School	APG (rank)	Season
Marcus Williams	Connecticut	7.8 (3rd)	2004–5
Jared Jordan (Hartford)	Marist	8.5 (1st)	2005–6
Jared Jordan (Hartford)	Marist	8.7 (1st)	2006–7

Field Goal Percentage

Player (hometown)	School	Pct. (rank)	Season
Toby Kimball	Connecticut	.569 (7th)	1964–65
Mark Young	Fairfield	.629 (6th)	1977–78
Phil Ness (Fairfield)	Lafayette	.617 (10th)	1977–78
Chuck Aleksinas (Litchfield)	Connecticut	.631 (10th)	1980–81
Pete DeBisschop (Cheshire)	Fairfield	.627 (9th)	1982–83
Sean Scott	Central Conn. State	.670 (2nd)	1996–97
David Tompkins	Yale	.600 (8th)	1998–99
Dominick Martin	Yale	.603 (8th)	2003–4
Emeka Okafor	Connecticut	.599 (9th)	2003–4
Kibwe Trim	Sacred Heart	.618 (9th)	2005–6
Joey Henley	Sacred Heart	.626 (3rd)	2008–9
Justin Rutty	Quinnipiac	.604 (10th)	2008–9

3-Point Field Goal Percentage

Player (hometown)	School	Pct. (rank)	Season
Albert Mouring	Connecticut	.478 (6th)	1999–2000

Free Throw Percentage

Player (hometown)	School	Pct. (rank)	Season
Tony Lavelli Jr.	Yale	.824 (6th)	1948–49
John Weber	Yale	.830 (1st)	1952–53
John Pipczynski	Connecticut	.836 (7th)	1959–60
Wes Bialosuknia	Connecticut	.859 (9th)	1966–67
Calvin Murphy (Norwalk)	Niagara	.881 (4th)	1969–70
Frank Oleynick (Bridgeport)	Seattle	.888 (1st)	1974–75
Joe DeSantis	Fairfield	.892 (6th)	1976–77
Wes Matthews (Bridgeport)	Wisconsin	.888 (6th)	1979–80
Rod Foster (New Britain)	UCLA	.950 (1st)	1981–82
Keith Webster (Monroe)	Harvard	.889 (10th)	1984–85
Ed Petersen	Yale	.888 (9th)	1988–89
Khalid El-Amin	Connecticut	.892 (4th, T)	1999–2000
Albert Mouring	Connecticut	.889 (8th, T)	2000–1
Tristan Blackwood	Central Conn. State	.924 (5th)	2006–7

Blocks Per Game

Player (hometown)	School	BPG (rank)	Season
Charles Smith (Bridgeport)	Pittsburgh	3.2 (8th)	1986–87
Charles Smith (Bridgeport)	Pittsburgh	3.1 (9th)	1987–88
Kenny Green (Waterbury)	Rhode Island	3.0 (8th)	1988–89
Kenny Green (Waterbury)	Rhode Island	4.8 (1st)	1989–90
Vin Baker (Old Saybrook)	Hartford	3.7 (5th)	1991–92
Marcus Camby (Hartford)	Massachusetts	3.6 (6th)	1993–94

Records

Player (hometown)	School	BPG (rank)	Season
Donyell Marshall	Connecticut	3.3 (8th)	1993–94
Keith Closs (Hartford)	Central Conn. State	5.3 (1st)	1994–95
Marcus Camby (Hartford)	Massachusetts	3.4 (10th)	1994–95
Keith Closs (Hartford)	Central Conn. State	6.4 (1st)	1995–96
Marcus Camby (Hartford)	Massachusetts	3.9 (7th)	1995–96
Emeka Okafor	Connecticut	4.1 (3rd)	2001–2
Deng Gai	Fairfield	4.0 (5th)	2001–2
Emeka Okafor	Connecticut	4.7 (1st)	2002–3
Deng Gai	Fairfield	3.8 (4th)	2002–3
Emeka Okafor	Connecticut	4.1 (2nd)	2003–4
Deng Gai	Fairfield	5.5 (1st)	2004–5
Josh Boone	Connecticut	2.9 (10th)	2004–5
Hilton Armstrong	Connecticut	3.1 (8th)	2005–6
Hasheem Thabeet	Connecticut	3.8 (3rd)	2006–7
Hasheem Thabeet	Connecticut	4.5 (3rd)	2007–8
Hasheem Thabeet	Connecticut	4.2 (2nd)	2008–9
Greg Mangano (Orange)	Yale	3.0 (9th)	2010–11

Steals Per Game

Player (hometown)	School	SPG (rank)	Season
Nadav Henefeld	Connecticut	3.7 (3rd)	1989–90
Scott Burrell (Hamden)	Connecticut	3.6 (2nd)	1990–91
David Corbitt	Central Conn. State	3.1 (3rd)	1991–92
Rick Mickens	Central Conn. State	3.6 (2nd)	1999–2000
Damian Saunders (Waterbury)	Duquesne	2.8 (2nd)	2009–10

NCAA Division II National Leaders

Player (hometown)	School	Category	Season
Don Perrelli (New Haven)	Southern Conn. St.	31.5 PPG	1959–60
Darrin Robinson (Bridgeport)	Sacred Heart	32.0 PPG	1992–93
Charlie Wrinn (Glastonbury)	Trinity	25.6 RPG	1951–52
Andre Means	Sacred Heart	16.1 RPG	1976–77
Rick Mahorn (Hartford)	Hampton	15.8 RPG	1979–80
Ramel Allen	Bridgeport	14.1 RPG	2004–5
Steve Ray	Bridgeport	12.5 APG	1988–89
Steve Ray	Bridgeport	11.7 APG	1989–90

Outstanding High School Performances

60 Points or More in a Game

78—Maurice Williamson, Wilbur Cross v. Westbury, L.I., 2/13/88, W 108–92 *(25-44 FG, 8 3s, 20-27 FT)*

71—Danny Moore, South Catholic v. Bullard-Havens, 2/13/70, W 110–85 *(30-55 FG, 11-15 FT)*

68—Harun Ramey, Crosby v. Wolcott, 2/13/90, W 103–39 *(26-34 FG, 3 3s, 13 FT)*

66—J. Alden White, Crosby v. Branford, 2/7/22, W 153–17 *(33 FG, 0-0 FT)*

64—Jim Fitzsimmons, Fairfield Prep v. Jonathan Law, 2/17/69, W 138–78 *(25-43 FG, 14-20 FT)*

62—Calvin Murphy, Norwalk v. Roger Ludlowe, 1/14/66, W 126–53 *(27-44 FG, 8-11 FT)*

61—Marcus Robinson, Wilby v. Wolcott, 2/19/93, W 141–56. *(20 FG, 11 3s, 10 FT)*

60—Wayne Lawrence, Stonington at St. Mary's, New Haven, 2/10/56, W 99–48 *(25 FG, 10 FT)*

60—Tom Roy, South Windsor v. Middletown, Class M state tournament semifinals, 3/12/70, W 103–54 *(26-28 FG, 8-10 FT)*

60—Earl Kelley, Wilbur Cross v. West Haven, 2/11/82, W 96–93 *(20-28 FG, 20-26 FT)*

60—Phil Lott, Wilby v. Kennedy, 2/26/88, W 107–80 *(23 FG, 7 3s, 7 FT)*

60—Chazz McCarter, Hillhouse v. Lyman Hall, 1/18/05, W 106–46 *(6 3s)*

Connecticut's 2,000-Point Career Scorers

2,691—Walter Luckett, Kolbe, Bridgeport, 1968–72

2,501—Tom Roy, South Windsor, 1968–71

2,491—Anthony Harris, Danbury, 1988–91

Records

Maurice Williamson, son of the late John Williamson, holds Connecticut's single-game high school scoring record with 78 points, achieving that figure with Wilbur Cross—his father's alma mater—in 1988. Maurice played three seasons at Louisiana State, where he teamed up with Shaquille O'Neal. *Courtesy of LSU Sports Information.*

2,357—Alex Jensen, Stonington, 1996–2000
2,301—Rashamel Jones, Trinity Catholic, Stamford, 1992–95
2,263—Matt Curtis, Cheshire, 1987–90
2,228—Jordan Williams, Torrington, 2006–9
2,212—Phil Lott, Wilby, Waterbury, 1985–88
2,192—Calvin Murphy, Norwalk, 1963–66
2,180—Stepfan Holley, Capital Prep, Hartford, 2006–9
2,174—John Pinone, South Catholic, Hartford, 1976–79
2,149—Dave Vigeant, Litchfield, 1976–79
2,124—Jerome Malloy, Kennedy, Waterbury, 1988–91
2,107—William "Frenchy" Tomlin, Warren Harding, Bridgeport, 1984–87
2,100—John Williamson, Wilbur Cross, New Haven, 1966–70
2,087—Edmund Saunders, Holy Cross, Waterbury, 1994–97
2,061—Sean Tabb, Somers, 1991–94

Most State Championships, Coaches

10—Vito Montelli, St. Joseph, Trumbull
9—Sam Bender, Hillhouse, New Haven
9—Charlie Bentley, Warren Harding, Bridgeport
9—Bob Saulsbury, Wilbur Cross, New Haven
6—Frank Crisafi, East Haven
6—Mike Walsh, Trinity Catholic, Stamford

Bibliography

BOOKS

Carter, Craig, and Alex Sachare. *Official NBA Register, 1993–94*. St. Louis, MO: Sporting News, 1993.

Davis, Ken. *University of Connecticut Basketball Vault*. Atlanta: Whitman Vault Books, 2010.

Douchant, Mike. *Inside Sports' College Basketball*. Detroit, MI: Visible Ink Press, 1997.

ESPN: College Basketball Encyclopedia. New York: Ballantine Books, 2009.

Gentile, John. *Encyclopedia of High School Basketball*. Torrington, CT: Gentile Publishing, 1969.

Jordan, Pat. *Chase the Game*. New York: Dodd, Mead, & Company, 1979.

Naismith, James. *Basketball: Its Origin and Development*. Lincoln: University of Nebraska Press, 1996.

NCAA. *2002 Men's NCAA Basketball Records*. Indianapolis, IN: National Collegiate Athletic Association, 2002.

Orton, Kathy. *Outside the Limelight: Basketball in the Ivy League*. New Brunswick, NJ: Rutgers University Press, 2009.

Sports Illustrated 2011 Almanac. New York: Time Home Entertainment, Inc., 2010.

PERIODICALS

Agostino, David. "His Own Man." *Connecticut Post*, February 25, 2000.

Anderson, Woody. "Hoop City: Success of Three Players Ignited Bridgeport Basketball Boom." *Hartford Courant*, January 31, 1989.

Birge, Bob. "Harding Legends Put City on Map." *Connecticut Post*, November 8, 1996.

Conner, Desmond. "Service a Celebration of Knight's Life." *Hartford Courant*, May 31, 2008.

Ehalt, Bob. "High School Basketball: Connecticut's Best." *Stamford Advocate*, February 17, 1991.

Elsberry, Chris. "Step Forward, and Back." *Connecticut Post*, December 16, 2009.

Goldstein, Richard. "Tony Lavelli, 71, Musician with a Memorable Hook Shot." *New York Times*, January 13, 1998.

Harrison, Don. "Corley Tallies 51 as UConn Breezes." *Waterbury Republican*, January 11, 1968.

———. "An Era Ends, by George." *Waterbury Republican*, March 15, 1968.

———. "Fairfield Tops Niagara, 88–85; Murphy Held to 28." *Waterbury Republican*, January 27, 1968.

———. "Kimball vs. Kimble." *Waterbury Republican*, December 3, 1964.

———. "Thompson Right, But Could be Wrong." *Waterbury American*, February 26, 1979.

———. "Wardlaw Feels Stuff Ban No Benefit to Basketball." *New Haven Journal-Courier*, March 30, 1967.

———. "When Perno Stole the Ball." *Waterbury Republican*, February 9, 1975.

Jacobs, Jeff. "Providence Has a Claim, Too." *Hartford Courant*, February 22, 2009.

Lewis, Mark A. "Easties' Streak May Be Struck." *New Haven Register*, March 26, 1978.

Litsky, Frank. "John Lee, 64, an Athlete at Yale Who Chose Industry over Knicks." *New York Times*, May 8, 2001.

Marslano, Paul. "Now THIS Was a Streak to Remember." *New Haven Register*, November 27, 1977.

Montville, Leigh. "A Gift From on High." *Sports Illustrated*, June 28, 2010.

———. "Mighty Mike." *Sports Illustrated*, January 20, 1992.

Raley, Dan. "Where Are They Now? John Castellani, Seattle U Basketball Coach." *Seattle Post-Intelligencer*, March 28, 2007.

Reveron, Derek. "Coaches' Tall Order: Capturing Big Tiger from the Cage Crop." *Wall Street Journal*, March 10, 1978.

Reynolds, Bill. "PC Once More Honors Its Past by Raising Johnny Egan's Name to the Rafters." *Providence Journal*, February 19, 2009.

Riley, Lori. "The Popular Choice of the Weaver Crowd." *Hartford Courant*, December 6, 1999.

Shriver, Timothy. "Getting Grief Right." *Washington Post*, February 18, 2008.

Sinicrope, Kathryn. "Attorney, Sportsman Broberg Dies at 81." *Palm Beach Daily News*, November 24, 2001.

Springer, Shira. "Gomes's New Home Is Move-in Ready." *Boston Globe*, September 28, 2005.

Sunday Herald. "Coombs to Lay Off for One Semester." July 8, 1956.

Wadley, George. "One of the Best Ended Up in the Worst Way." *New Haven Register*, September 25, 1989.

Wiley, Ralph. "A Master of Intimidation." *Sports Illustrated*, April 10, 1989.

Wise, Michael. "Camby Gives Back as He Gets Away." *New York Times*, December 23, 2001.

WEBSITES

Basketball-Reference.com.

Sports-Reference.com.

About the Author

As a sportswriter, Don Harrison was passionate about college basketball, baseball and Yale football—often in that sequence. And so he is pleased to present this collection of his works, and some new material, that provide valuable insight into the state of Connecticut's myriad contributions to the game of basketball, from the rarefied heights of the NBA and UConn to the high schools and playgrounds.

Don spent more evenings and afternoons than he can recall covering basketball for the *Waterbury Republican*, *Waterbury American* and *New Haven Journal-Courier*. He also wrote about the game and its participants for the *Sporting News*, the *New York Times*, the *Basketball Times*, two university magazines, *Fairfield Now* and *Sacred Heart*, and other publications.

Don was a contributing author to *Inside Women's College Basketball: Anatomy of a Season* and its successor, *Inside Women's College Basketball: Anatomy of Two Seasons*. As a young sports editor who chronicled the rise of Fairfield University men's basketball in the early 1970s, he had the chutzpah (if limited business acumen) to publish and author the book *25 Years Plus One*.

During his tenure in Waterbury, he won two Connecticut Sportswriter of the Year Awards from the National Sportscasters and Sportswriters Association. His cover story for the *Fairfield County Advocate*, "The Devil Drives," was cited in *The Best American Sportswriting 1993*.

Away from the sports arena, Don was the founding editor of the *Greenwich Citizen*, a weekly newspaper that garnered several awards— including one for General Excellence—from the New England Press Association and the Connecticut Press Club. He is a contributing columnist to two news websites, Fairfield Patch and Naugatuck Patch.

Don and his wife, Patti, reside in Fairfield, Connecticut.